THE ART OF PROGRAMMING
THE ZX SPECTRUM

...nes, B.Sc., M.B.C.S.

BERNARD BABANI (publishing) LTD
THE GRAMPIANS
SHEPHERDS BUSH ROAD
LONDON W6 7NF
ENGLAND

Although every care has been taken with the preparation of this book, the publishers or author will not be held responsible in any way for any errors that might occur.

© 1983 BERNARD BABANI (publishing) LTD

First Published – February 1983
Reprinted – January 1984

British Library Cataloguing in Publication Data
    James, M.
        The art of programming the ZX Spectrum.
        1. Sinclair ZX Spectrum (Computer) – Programming
        I. Title
        001.64'2   QA76.8.S625

    ISBN 0 85934 094 5

Printed and bound in Great Britain by
Cox & Wyman Ltd, Reading

PREFACE

Whether you are fairly new to computing or a seasoned programmer you are likely to have lots of questions on the theme of "How can I program my Spectrum to do . . . ?" This book is designed to give you some of the answers. It aims to teach you programming techniques that turn straightforward BASIC into really effective programs.

This book introduces all the features of the Spectrum you need to write games programs that are fun to watch and exciting to play. Chapter Two introduces low resolution colour graphics. Chapter Three explains how to use the random number generator and we return to graphics, this time in high resolution, in Chapter Four. Chapter Five explores the Spectrum's sound capabilities. Dynamic Graphics is the subject of Chapter Six while Chapter Seven explains two very powerful commands, PEEK and POKE. Chapter Eight is devoted to the Spectrum's internal timing mechanism and in Chapter Nine we take a look at its facilities for string handling. Finally, in Chapter Ten, graphics is again the topic under consideration, this time at a rather advanced level.

You might think that by the time all this had been covered we'd be running out of new information about the Spectrum. Not at all — there's a great deal to the Spectrum, much more than you'd ever imagine from its compact size.

M. James

This book is dedicated to my parents,
Mr and Mrs R. James,
who were responsible for starting my program

CONTENTS

Chapter One

GETTING TO KNOW YOUR SPECTRUM

The Sinclair Spectrum presents its users with a really marvellous deal. It allows versatile use of colour, offers both high resolution and low resolution graphics, and also adds sound. The result can mean some very effective and exciting programs from BASIC — if you just know how. The trouble is that there is a little more than meets the eye in getting your Spectrum to do clever things. It's one thing to have learned how to use all the Spectrum's commands, and a very different one to be able to combine them into programs that do exactly what you want them to. And that's just what this book aims to teach you: it sets out to give you the knack of effective programming with your Spectrum.

An exciting prospect

We'll look in more detail at each of the Spectrum's special features as we progress through this book, so you'll find that the Spectrum's colour and its low resolution graphics are the subject of Chapter Two, its facility for high resolution graphics is explored in Chapter Four, and its sound is explained in Chapter Five.

Lots of home computers now have colour and sound so what's so special about the Spectrum? Well, for a start the fact that it has both low-res and hi-res graphics is a great advantage. On the whole, low-res graphics is faster to use and more convenient but there are things — like drawing fine outline lines and shapes — that are only possible in hi-res graphics. Combining both in the same program, you can create a much greater range of displays than using either alone. Secondly, the Spectrum's colour is very accommodating. There are some restrictions relating to the use of colour with high resolution graphics, but with low resolution graphics you can mix your colours fairly freely on the screen. Thirdly, the Spectrum uses a version of BASIC that has some very useful facilities — which will be introduced in the course of this book — and helps you to write programs easily by providing you with all the keywords. It even notices lots of your programming mistakes as you make them — and this is a great advantage.

Artful programming

This book aims to help you write your own programs. As such it's not a complete introduction to BASIC or to the Spectrum. So, before you go very far into it you'll need to be used to using the Spectrum's keyboard to write some simple BASIC programs.

Let's assume that you've dipped into the manual that came with your Spectrum and have learned enough about the machine to have no trouble getting it running, and have learned enough about BASIC to be able to read and write short programs. You may still not be in a position to translate the ideas in your head into actual Spectrum programs. This is because there is more to programming than knowing BASIC — just as there is more to English than being able to pronounce a few words.

This is where this book comes in. It tries to show you how to use programming techniques and the features of the Spectrum to convert ideas into actuality. In other words, it demonstrates how to build up programs in fairly easy stages, adding extra features as you learn how to use them. The book contains lots of snippets of programs but there are also more than twenty fully-fledged games programs that are fun to play with — after all, you'll want a break from programming every now and again and it's also nice to be able to demonstrate just how clever you and your Spectrum can be! However, even the "complete" programs can be improved upon — there's never such a thing as the perfect program. So as you play the games, try to see how they could be developed further and then try out your ideas. It's much easier to learn through adding to an existing program than starting from scratch!

Learning and fun

Most of the programs in this book could loosely be described as games programs. From a quick glance at the Contents page you might be a little surprised by this and might wonder at the absence of "serious" programs. One reason for concentrating on games is that such programs can be designed to demonstrate all the facilities of the Spectrum. Another is to make learning an enjoyable process. We probably learn faster and better if we are having fun at the same time. It's important not to think of games in terms of nonsense. The dividing line between sheer fun and the serious pursuit of knowledge is a very blurred one as far as computers are concerned. After all, today's spaceship games were developed from programs that really were used to put men and spacecraft into orbit and land them on the Moon.

Your Spectrum system

This book has been written using a 16K Spectrum, a TV set, a cassette recorder, and the illustrations have been produced using a ZX Printer. This means that the programs included will run on any Spectrum – a 16K or the more powerful 48K. The Spectrum is a colour computer but if you are using a black and white TV you will still be able to appreciate many of the effects of colour displays – which will be seen as different shades of grey. However, there are some colour combinations, for example, red and green, that do not show up at all well in black and white – so experiment and stick to colours that contrast well with each other. Once you've entered programs from this book, or written your own programs, you can save them either on cassette tape or, using a Sinclair ZX Microdrive, on micro-floppies. If you want to try out the programs without having to type them in for yourself, you will be pleased to know that you can buy a cassette tape that includes many of the complete programs in this book from "Ramsoft" – you'll find further details on the last page of this book.

Chapter Two

LOW RESOLUTION GRAPHICS

The Spectrum has only one display mode but it has two different ways of changing the contents of the screen. In other words, the Spectrum uses the same method to display text and graphics. Broadly speaking, the two ways that ZX BASIC allows you to modify the screen give rise to two different ways of thinking about graphics — high resolution and low resolution. It is important to realise that these are only different ways of *thinking* because the Spectrum really only has one way of producing a screen display.

The Spectrum's screen

The Spectrum's screen can be thought of as composed of a grid of 256 (horizontal) by 176 (vertical) dots. Any of these dots can either be "on" or "off" and shapes — letters, digits, etc — can be made from patterns of "on" dots or "off" dots. The only thing that is missing from this description is exactly what is meant by "on" and "off". To make things simple let's just consider a case where only two colours are involved. For even greater simplicity, and for those without a colour TV, let's consider the case of black and white. If "on" dots show on the screen as black and "off" dots show as white then you can see that the above description makes sense. If you form the shape of a letter in "on" dots surrounded by "off" dots then the letter will show up as black on white. The similarity between using black or "on" dots to write on a white background and ordinary writing prompts the use of the terms "ink" dots and "paper" dots rather than "on" and "off".

To summarise, the Spectrum's screen is made up of two different types of dot — ink dots and paper dots. In general the ink dots show up as one colour and the paper dots show up as another. The Spectrum has two commands that allow the setting of the colour of the ink and paper dots to be set.

4

INK 'colour'

and

PAPER 'colour'

assign the colour corresponding to the number "colour" to the ink and paper dots respectively. There is no need to remember which numbers correspond to which colours because the colours are written above the top row of number keys on the Spectrum. For completeness, however, they are:

0 – Black
1 – Blue
2 – Red
3 – Magenta
4 – Green
5 – Cyan
6 – Yellow
7 – White

Thus the command INK 2 will make all the ink dots show as red and the command PAPER 6 will make all the paper dots show as yellow. The setting of the ink and paper colours is entirely independent. Notice that there is nothing stopping you from defining the ink and paper colours to be the same, e.g. INK 4 followed by PAPER 4 will make both ink and paper dots show as green. In this case of course, you will not be able to see the difference between ink and paper dots (they are both the same colour) but it is important to realise that there are still two different types of dot.

If you have been following this discussion then you will be wondering how it is possible for the Spectrum to display more than two colours at a time. The answer to this question is that the screen is divided up into a number of small square areas, each only eight dots by eight dots, called "character locations". Within each character location it is possible to specify the colour of the ink and paper dots independently. This may seem like a strange idea, but in fact it makes the Spectrum very easy to use. The eight-by-eight square is, in fact, more than enough to display letters, digits and many of the small shapes that are of use in games etc. This makes it convenient to deal with the screen in terms of character locations and indeed this is exactly what the PRINT statement does. Each time you use a PRINT statement to print a character on the screen what you are doing is defining which dots within an eight-by-eight square will be paper dots and which will be ink dots. The colour of the ink and paper dots can be set for each individual character location.

The use of PRINT statements to change the contents of character locations to make pictures (perhaps including text) is known as low resolution graphics. The Spectrum also has a set of commands that allow the changing of a single dot from paper to ink or vice versa. These commands lead us into the area of high resolution graphics. The only trouble is that we are still restricted to a single ink and a single paper colour within each character location. This results in some interesting difficulties when it comes to trying to use high resolution "full colour" graphics. Because of these and other difficulties most Spectrum programs achieve their effects mainly by the use of low resolution graphics. In the rest of this chapter we consider the details of low resolution graphics and in Chapter Four look at the other side of the coin, high resolution graphics.

The PRINT command — comma, semicolon and apostrophe

The general form of a PRINT statement is:

    PRINT 'print list'

where "print list" is a list of items to be printed, separated by either commas, semicolons or apostrophes. The different separators have different effects on the way the print items are actually placed on the screen. For example, a semicolon results in no space being left between the items when they are printed on the screen. That is:

    PRINT "a";"b"

will print ab on the screen without leaving any space between the two letters. The effects that the three separators have can be summarised as:

6

Separator		effect
semicolon	;	leave no space between print items
comma	,	move to the next print zone before printing the next item
apostrophe	'	move to the start of the next line before printing the next item

The only term in this table that needs further explanation is "print zone". The Spectrum's screen is split into two print zones. The first extends from column 1 to column 16 and the second from 17 to 32. Thus:

```
PRINT "a","b"
```

will print a at the beginning of a line and b in the 17th column.

There is one important extra point about using separators. If you end a PRINT statement with *any* separator then the usual starting of a new line at the end of the print statement is suppressed. In other words:

```
10 PRINT "a"
20 PRINT "b"
```

places a and b at the start of two different lines but

```
10 PRINT "a",
20 PRINT "b"
```

has the same effect as

```
10 PRINT "a","b"
```

The most important application of this fact is in the ending of a PRINT statement with a semicolon. This results in the next PRINT statement continuing by printing the first item right after the last item of the original PRINT statement. For example:

```
10 PRINT "a";
20 GOTO 10
```

will fill the screen with letter As. One strange effect of the rule that a separator at the end of a line suppresses the starting of a

7

new line is demonstrated by

10 PRINT "a"'

Ending a PRINT statement with an apostrophe results in no change. The reason for this is that the fact that there is a separator at the end of the statement stops the automatic starting of a new line! Thus if you want to leave a one line space use either PRINT or PRINT '. If you want to leave two lines use PRINT ' ' etc.

PRINT TAB and AT

Although the careful use of the comma and the semicolon can handle most of our printing problems, it is difficult using them alone to place something exactly where you want it on the screen. This problem can be overcome by use of the TAB function. If you use TAB(N) in a PRINT statement the next thing to be printed will appear at column N on the current line. If the PRINT statement has already gone beyond column N then the next thing to be printed will appear at column N of the NEXT line. To show this try the following program:

10 PRINT TAB(25);"ab";TAB(25);"ab"

Notice that, although you could use a comma after the TAB command, it wouldn't be useful because it would move the print position on from where the TAB left it! If you use a value of N bigger than 32, then 32 is subtracted from it repeatedly until it's in the correct range.

All of the PRINT commands that we have used so far have the limitation that they only allow positioning within the current line but there is a command, PRINT AT, that will let you print anything anywhere.

The AT command is very easy to use:

PRINT AT Y,X;"WORD"

will print WORD at line Y and column X. If there is already something printed at row Y and column X this makes no difference. WORD replaces it. The Spectrum's screen is 32 characters wide by 22 lines high. The first row is at the top of the screen and is numbered 0. The first column of characters is on the left-hand side of the screen and is also numbered zero. This means that X must lie between 0 and 31 and Y must lie between 0 and 21. If X or Y are outside of their proper ranges then the error message "Integer out of range" will be displayed. For a simple example of PRINT AT try:

```
10 PRINT AT 11,16;"*"
```

which will print an asterisk in the middle of the screen. You can use PRINT AT to draw simple shapes on the screen. For example,

```
10 FOR i=0 TO 31
20 PRINT AT 10,i;"*"
30 NEXT i
40 FOR i=0 TO 21
50 PRINT AT i,15;"*"
60 NEXT i
```

will print a horizontal and a vertical line of asterisks. You can use as many ATs in a PRINT statement as you like.

Graphics characters

The previous example shows how PRINT AT can be used to draw shapes on the screen rather than just print information at particular locations. However, making shapes with asterisks and letters is hardly good looking graphics. To help the situation the Spectrum provides a number of special "graphics characters". Twenty-one of these can be defined by the user and these will be discussed later. There are, however, sixteen pre-defined graphics that can be used to make a limited range of shapes without going to any extra trouble.

The sixteen graphics characters can be seen printed on the top row of keys. To be more precise, you can see eight of the sixteen printed on the top row of keys and the remaining eight are simply their "inverse", i.e. the same eight shapes but black becomes white and vice versa. To obtain these extra graphics characters all that is necessary is to change to "graphics" mode by pressing CAPS SHIFT and the GRAPHICS key (the 9 key on the top row) at the same time. This changes the letter in the flashing cursor to a "G" and then pressing any of the top row of keys with graphics characters printed on produces that graphics character on the screen. The other eight characters are produced by also pressing the CAPS SHIFT key while still in graphics mode. It is a good idea to actually try this out to make sure that you understand the idea and can actually produce all sixteen graphics characters. It is important to notice that the "inverse" set of eight graphics characters are distinctly different characters from the first eight. This might seem like an obvious point but later on we will see that there is a way to print *any* character as an "inverse". To get out of graphics mode all you have to do is press the GRAPHICS key once more.

Because of the difficulty in reproducing Spectrum (or any) graphics characters in print we will indicate graphics characters by placing square brackets around the letter or digit on the key that you would have to press to produce the graphics character. So for example [3] means the graphics character that you get by pressing the "three" key while in graphics mode. In addition an up arrow "^" should be taken to mean "press the key while pressing CAPS SHIFT at the same time". So that [^3] is the graphics character that you get if you press the "three" key and CAPS SHIFT while in graphics mode.

Because of the limited number of shapes present among the sixteen graphics they aren't as useful as you might think. You can use them for drawing shapes such as squares etc. by PRINTing the correct combination but their main use lies in making up small solid shapes for use in games etc. For example, if you want to PRINT a "dog" shape on the screen you might try.

10 PRINT "[1][^1][^3]"'"[8][^5][5]"

How to make the dog move around the screen will be described in Chapter Six.

The trouble with the sixteen supplied graphics characters is that if you want to draw a shape such as a square or a circle then this can usually be better achieved by using high resolution graphics and if you want to make a solid shape such as the "dog" then this is better done via the "user-defined" graphics characters (described later). However, this said, it is always worth looking at the supplied graphics characters to see if one will do the job. They are particularly useful for example, for drawing thick horizontal or vertical lines. Try:

```
10 FOR i=1 TO 32
20 PRINT "[3]";
30 NEXT i
40 FOR i=1 TO 31
50 PRINT TAB(16);"[5]"
60 NEXT i
```

Notice the use of the TAB and the semicolon to position the graphics characters on the screen.

CHR$

There is another way of producing graphics or any other sort of character — the CHR$ function. If you imagine all of the Spectrum's characters written out in order then you could pick out a single character by saying something like "the 36th character". This is exactly what the CHR$ function does. CHR$(36) is the 36th character in the Spectrum's set of characters. If you want to see all of your Spectrum's character set then try:

```
10 FOR i=32 TO 255
20 PRINT CHR$(i);
30 FOR j=1 TO 100
40 NEXT j
50 NEXT i
```

You will notice that sometimes a single letter is printed and sometimes a whole word — such as COPY or PRINT. The Spectrum treats all of the BASIC words that you type in with a single keypress as a single symbol.

The most important thing about CHR$ function is that it

11

provides a link between number and characters. As an example of how this can be used try the following program:

```
10 PRINT CHR$(INT(RND*16+128));
20 GOTO 10
```

This will fill the screen with random graphics characters. The exact way this program works will become clear after the next chapter where the use of the RND function is explained. However, the role of the CHR$ function converting numbers to characters should be clear if you try running the same program but with the CHR$ function left out!

User-defined graphics characters

There is no doubt that the feature that makes the Spectrum's low resolution graphics useful is the ability to define new characters. This is relatively easy to do and effectively increases the level of detail that is possible in low resolution graphics. Not only is it easy to define new characters; once they are defined they can be used just like any other existing character.

You may be wondering where these extra characters are lurking? If you enter graphics mode and press any of the keys between A and U in the alphabet then you might be surprised at seeing the appropriate letters between A and U printed on the screen. It looks as though there are two ways to produce these particular letters — normally and in graphics mode. The reason for this is that the graphics characters produced by this set of keys are initially set to the shapes of the letters of the alphabet. How to change their definition to something more useful is the subject of this section!

The first problem that we have to solve is how to specify the shape of the character in terms of ink and paper dots. One way of doing this is to represent a paper dot by "0" (zero) and an ink dot by "1". So for example, if you wanted to define a "dog" you might use the following pattern of 0's and 1's.

```
1 1 0 0 0 0 0 1
1 1 0 0 0 0 1 0
0 0 1 1 1 1 1 0
0 0 1 1 1 1 1 0
0 0 1 1 0 1 1 0
0 1 1 0 0 0 1 1
0 0 0 0 0 0 0 0
0 0 0 0 0 0 0 0
```

Remember that a character uses an eight-by-eight square of dots. If you have difficulty seeing the shape of a dog in the above square of ones and zeros then try copying it out and colour the ones black. Once you have understood this method of forming a pattern of noughts and ones, you should be able to see how to go about defining any shape that you want.

The next problem is to transfer this definition to the user-defined character that will produce it. As already mentioned the user-defined characters are associated with the keys "a" to "u". The definition of the character produced by these keys when they are pressed in graphics mode is stored in the Spectrum's memory a row at a time. To change the definition of a row of any particular character we need to use a fairly complicated statement. For example, if we want to change the definition of the 3rd row of the letter "B" you have to use:

POKE USR "b"+2,BIN xxxxxxx

where the xxxxxxxx is replaced by the row of noughts and ones that you want. It's not necessary to understand the working of this line of BASIC to define new characters. The only thing to notice is that the rows are numbered from 0 to 7 so in the above example the third row is altered by using "b+2" after USR. In general, to alter the nth row of character C to xxxxxxxx use.

POKE USR "C"+n-1,BIN xxxxxxx

To define a complete character it is of course necessary to define all eight new rows.

Although it's not necessary to understand the workings of the above statement to define new characters it is interesting. (You can skip this paragraph on first reading.) The function USR "letter" returns the address of the memory location used to store the first row of the graphics character corresponding to "letter". Thus,

USR "letter"+1

is the address of the second row and so on. The function BIN converts the row of noughts and ones to a number. To see this try:

10 PRINT BIN 011

with different rows of noughts and ones. The conversion is actually done by treating the row as a binary number and hence the name of the function. This resulting number is then stored in the correct memory location by the POKE command. This is explained in Chapter Seven. This number stored in the correct memory location produces the required pattern of ink and paper dots when the Spectrum prints the graphics character.

As an example of a user-defined graphics character we return to our dog:

```
10 POKE USR "a"+0,BIN 11000001
20 POKE USR "a"+1,BIN 11000010
30 POKE USR "a"+2,BIN 00111110
40 POKE USR "a"+3,BIN 00111110
50 POKE USR "a"+4,BIN 00110110
60 POKE USR "a"+5,BIN 01100011
70 POKE USR "a"+6,BIN 00000000
80 POKE USR "a"+7,BIN 00000000
90 PRINT "[A]"
```

This program first defines the new character in lines 10 to 80 and then prints it in line 90. After the program has run the new definition of [A] remains until the Spectrum is switched off or until it is redefined. To see that this is true simply try pressing the "A" key while in graphics mode.

14

The way is now open to space ships, rockets, ships, tanks etc. and we will return to user-defined graphics again and again in the rest of this book.

Using colour

The basic method of controlling colour on the Spectrum has already been introduced — the INK and PAPER commands. However, there are a few things about the exact way that these work that haven't been discussed. The first point is that an INK or PAPER command sets the colour of all the ink and paper dots printed *after* the command. That is, INK and PAPER do not affect the colour of any dots already on the screen. For example, try the following:

```
10 INPUT "Paper Colour ? ";p
20 INPUT "Ink Colour ? ";i
30 PAPER p
40 INK i
50 FOR j=1 TO 32
60 PRINT "X";
70 NEXT j
80 GOTO 10
```

After entering the paper and ink colour a whole line of Xs is printed in the specified colours. Notice that, although each new line on the screen comes up in the new colours, the old lines are left unaltered. (If you're using a black and white set the colours will be displayed as shades of grey.) While you are running this program it is worth trying out the effect of specifying the same ink and paper colour — remembers the Xs are still there!

This method of controlling colour is very easy to use but it is a little awkward if you want to print a number of things in different colours on the same line. This can be done by placing INK and PAPER commands in the PRINT statement. For example,

```
10 PRINT INK 0;PAPER 7;"X";INK 7;PAPER 0;"X"
```

prints a black X on a white background and then a white X on a black background. The most important thing to understand about using INK and PAPER commands in PRINT statements is that their effect is temporary and lasts only until the end of the PRINT statement. At the end of the PRINT command the the ink and paper colours return to what they were before the PRINT was carried out.

There are two other commands that are essential to the use of colour — CLS and BORDER. The CLS command simply clears the screen but it is worth being exact about what it does. CLS actually changes all the dots on the screen into paper dots and this means the whole screen takes on the current colour set by PAPER. The command BORDER simply sets the colour of the border that surrounds the part of the display that the Spectrum can print on. The only extra thing to note about BORDER is that it also controls the colour of the area of the screen where input happens. As an example of using CLS and BORDER try:

```
10 FOR i=0 TO 7
20 PAPER i
30 CLS
40 BORDER 7-i
50 PAUSE 5
60 NEXT i
```

If you want to see the colours change more slowly increase the number following the PAUSE command.

As a final example of using colours the following program prints a series of coloured bars.

```
10 FOR c=0 TO 7
20 PAPER c
30 PRINT "    ";:REM 4 spaces
40 NEXT c
50 GOTO 10
```

INVERSE and OVER

The two commands INVERSE and OVER are special in that they both affect the way characters are placed on the screen. The command INVERSE 1 results in all the following characters being produced on the screen with their ink dots replaced by paper dots and vice versa. To return to the normal mode of operation it is necessary to use the command INVERSE 0. Notice that INVERSE doesn't produce any new characters or change any existing definitions; it simply swaps paper and ink dots when the character is printed on the screen. To see the effect of INVERSE try the following:

```
10 INVERSE 1
20 INPUT a$
30 PRINT a$
40 GOTO 20
```

After running this program enter INVERSE 0 to return to normality.

The command OVER 1 also changes the way ink and paper dots are produced on the screen but in a way that is much more difficult to describe than in the case of INVERSE. Following OVER 1; what appears on the screen when you print a character depends on what is already on the screen. The rule is that if the old dot and the new dot are the same then the result is a paper dot. If the two dots are different, however, then the result is an ink dot. This may seem complicated but essentially it means that if you print a new character in the same place as an existing character then the two characters will both appear on the screen but where they cross over they "cancel out". For example:

```
10 CLS
20 OVER 1
30 PRINT AT 0,0;"A"
40 PRINT AT 0,0;"_"
50 PRINT AT 1,0;"A"
60 PRINT AT 1,0;"\"
70 OVER 0
```

The first print statement places the letter A in the top left hand corner. The second PRINT statement prints an underline character in the same spot. Because of the OVER 1 command in line 20 both characters appear together. However, lines 50 and 60 print the letter A and \ in the same place and although they both appear on the screen at the same time if you look carefully you should be able to see that where they meet there are paper dots.

One very special use of OVER is the printing and erasing of a single character. For example, if you print a message on the screen you can make it vanish by printing it a second time following OVER 1.

```
10 CLS
20 PRINT AT 0,0;"A message"
30 OVER 1
40 GOTO 20
```

If you run this program you will see that the message flashes as it appears and then disappears from the screen. The effect of both OVER 1 and INVERSE 1 last until either they are countered by OVER 0 and INVERSE 0 or until the machine is switched off, so beware. Like INK and PAPER, INVERSE and OVER can also be used within PRINT statements and their effect is then temporary. We will meet both INVERSE and OVER again in the chapter on high resolution graphics.

BRIGHT and FLASH – attributes

The final two commands that apply to the production of characters on the screen are like INK and PAPER in that they do not affect the pattern of ink and paper dots that appears on the screen in any way. Instead, they alter the way the ink and paper dots are displayed on the screen. Following BRIGHT 1, all the ink and paper dots are displayed at an increased level of brightness. Following FLASH 1, all the ink and paper dots are displayed as flashing, i.e. alternating between the ink and paper colour. Once again, to undo the effects it is necessary to use BRIGHT 0 and FLASH 0. To see the effects of these two commands try the following:

```
10 CLS
20 PAPER 1
30 INK 7
40 PRINT "This is normal"
50 BRIGHT 1
60 PRINT "This is bright"
70 BRIGHT 0
80 FLASH 1
90 PRINT "This is flashing"
100 BRIGHT 1
110 PRINT "This is bright and flashing"
120 BRIGHT 0
130 FLASH 0
```

Notice that you can use BRIGHT and FLASH together to produce bright flashing characters.

When you print a character on the screen the only thing that determines what it looks like is the pattern of ink and paper dots and the way that the individual ink and paper dots appear on the screen. Defining new graphics characters and using the commands INVERSE and OVER are the only ways of influencing the pattern of dots that appears on the screen. The commands INK, PAPER, FLASH and BRIGHT all effect the way that individual dots are displayed on the screen. In fact, this way of thinking mirrors the way that the Spectrum actually handles the screen display. One area of memory is used to store the pattern of dots and a separate area of memory holds the way each dot should be displayed. The way each dot is displayed is known as its "attributes" and the second area of memory is thus known as the "attributes area". We will return to the subject of attributes later, in Chapter Ten.

The attribute 8 and the colour 9

It is often the case that you would like to print something on the screen keeping the attributes of the character location the same. If you know what they are then there is no problem. All you have to do is to use the correct list of attribute commands, e.g. if you know a location is flashing then use FLASH 1 before printing to it. However, if you don't know what attributes are present then you are in difficulty unless you know about attribute 8. Using 8 in any of the attribute commands, i.e. BRIGHT, FLASH, INK, PAPER results in any characters added to the screen retaining the attributes of the character they replace. For example, following FLASH 8, any new characters printed will flash if they occupy a location that was flashing and will be steady otherwise. Following PAPER 8, any new characters will take on the paper colour of the character they replace. This sort of behaviour has resulted in attribute 8 being referred to as "transparent" in the sense that it lets the original attribute show through.

A related problem sometimes occurs with ink or paper colours. If you want to print something on the screen using the current paper colour, what ink colour should be used to make absolutely sure that it shows up. For example, if the current paper colour is black, you most certainly would not want to print using black ink! Once again, if you know the current paper colour, there is no problem — you simply choose a contrasting ink colour. However, if you don't know or if the colour varies, then there is a problem. This problem is solved by use of the "false" colour code 9. This simply means use a colour to contrast with the colour already in use. So, for example, INK 9 will select black if the current paper colour is light, i.e. 4 to 7; and white if the current paper colour is dark, i.e. 0 to 3. The same is true of PAPER 9, but in this case the colour is selected by contrast with the current ink colour. By using "colour" code 9 you can always be sure that things will show up on the screen but it is worth noticing that in practice 9 turns out to be either black or white and this can produce some very dull displays.

Conclusion

In this chapter we have looked at the fundamental ways in which the Spectrum's screen can be manipulated. Although no really impressive programs have been introduced in this

20

chapter it is difficult to go any further without such knowledge and the techniques of low resolution graphics will reappear and be developed in the remainder of this book.

Chapter Three

FUN AT RANDOM

In the abstract, randomness is rather an esoteric subject so it may come as a surprise to find it included in a book about games programming. However, when you think about it, randomness, or chance, is a fundamental component of games of all sorts. For a start there are games of chance — games with cards or dice; then there are games in which the speed with which you react to a chance event counts; and then there are games in which you use your skill to beat an opponent whose decisions you cannot predict in advance. Random numbers are at the heart of all these games.

Pseudo randomness!

What is a random number? Well, we've already hinted at the answer: it is a number which you could not possibly have predicted. The toss of a coin is random, so is the fall of a dice. You cannot know in advance whether the coin will fall as "heads" or as "tails". Neither can you say which face of the dice will fall uppermost and there is no way you can control the outcome. It is the fact that the players cannot influence the result that is the important aspect of a random event as far as game playing is concerned.

You may already be questioning whether a computer can ever produce a random number — after all, it can only output a function of what has previously been input. Well, the sceptics are, in this case, correct — a computer cannot give you a truly random number. A computer can only produce numbers that it calculates. The most important feature that we use about randomness is that the next outcome, or number, is unpredictable. We can make the computer calculate a set of numbers such that it is very difficult to predict the next number that comes up. Such a set of numbers is said to be "pseudo random".

To clarify matters, a pseudo-random number is one that is not produced by a random event (such as the throw of a dice). It is therefore theoretically predictable, but it can, for all practical purposes, be generated in such a way that no on-looker could ever work out what to expect next. In this sense we could say that the computer generates unpredictable numbers rather than random ones.

A computer generates its random numbers by using a formula and so anybody who has a copy of the formula can predict the next number in the sequence. However, in practice the formula is sufficiently complicated that for the purpose of playing games, where everything happens quickly, you'd need to be a mathematical genius to apply the formula in time.

RND and RAND

The Spectrum uses the function RND to produce pseudo-random numbers in the range 0 to 1. Every time you use the word RND the Spectrum calculates the next number in the sequence. Perhaps now you will not be too worried by the idea of the next random number being calculated! The numbers that RND calculates have one other very important characteristic — every number between 0 and 1 has approximately the same chance of being produced. Another, and more technical way of saying this, is to say that RND produces "uniformly distributed" pseudo-random numbers between 0 and 1.

Now that you understand what is going on when you use the RND function, let's see how to use it. To demonstrate the sort of output you get when you just ask for a random number type:

```
10 PRINT RND
20 GOTO 10
RUN
```

You will get a screen of numbers all lying between 0 and 1. For example,

```
.0011291504
.08581543
```

Are you struck by a coincidence? Have we just predicted the two numbers at the top of your screen? If not, turn your machine off and on again, and then try. Now your screen should display a list starting with those very numbers. The reason this happens is that the sequence of random numbers is generated by the same formula for all our machines — and the formula itself is given in the manual so it's no secret! If you RUN the program more than once without switching off between times, the sequence will simply continue from the place it was at before.

The fact that the random sequence is absolutely repeatable is actually very useful for some applications — for example, for testing alternative simulations where you want to repeat the same pattern of chance events — but for other purposes it is entirely worthless. Playing games of chance with your Spectrum would soon lose its attraction if it was not for the RAND function. (The Spectrum actually displays the word RANDOMIZE on the screen when you press the key marked RAND. To make the programs easier to type in, we will use RAND rather than RANDOMIZE.) The RAND function gives an instruction to the computer where to start in the sequence. This can either be a set point or it can be a chance point — equivalent to sticking a pin in a list. To predetermine the starting point you type

RAND any number

Try for example:

```
10 RAND 35
20 PRINT RND
30 GOTO 20
```

Try this a few times. The sequence is always the same. If you try

```
10 RAND 35
20 PRINT RND
30 GOTO 10
```

you will find that you keep on printing the same number — the starting point of the sequence given by RAND 35!

To get a different sequence each time use

10 RAND 0

When you use RAND 0 what actually happens is that the computer uses the value in an internal counter that counts the number of TV pictures displayed since you switched your machine on (see Chapter Eight). Although where the sequence begins is actually related to the time your machine has been switched on, the fact that the counter operates at a speed of 50 counts per second means that it is virtually impossible to predict its position when you type RAND 0. To recap all we have learned so far: the RND function calculates the next random number in the sequence, we can use RAND to set the starting point of the sequence in a way that is about as near to random as we can manage. To prove this try.

```
10 RAND 0
20 PRINT RND
30 GOTO 10
```

This will print out a set of starting points selected by RAND 0. You should see that although the starting value is increasing with time, it is almost impossible to predict. Thus, the most random, i.e. unpredictable series of numbers that your Spectrum can produce is given by.

```
10 RAND 0
20 PRINT RND
30 GOTO 20
```

Making things happen

On the face of it, the string of numbers that comes up on the screen when we ask for a random number, does not seem very useful. So let's take a simple application and see how to get the sort of results we want. Consider tossing a coin. There are two possibilities, "heads" and "tails". How do we simplify the raw output from the RND function to give one of these two answers and to give them fairly, i.e. with equal probability of the coin landing on either "heads" or "tails"? The solution is to split the range of answers into two exactly equal halves.

As the range goes from 0 to 1, this is easy. The halfway point is .5:

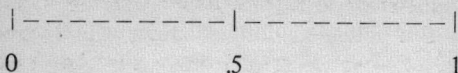

```
|— — — — — — — —|— — — — — — — —|
0              .5             1
```

As the numbers produced by RND are equally likely to fall anywhere on the line, half of them will fall below .5 and half will fall above .5. If we call a number that falls below .5 "heads" and one that falls above .5 "tails", then you can see that we will get as many heads as tails. Translating this into a program gives.

```
10 RAND 0
20 LET r=RND
30 IF r<.5 THEN PRINT "heads"
40 IF r>=.5 THEN PRINT "tails"
50 GOTO 20
```

At line 10 we randomise the starting point of the random numbers. At line 20 we get a random number into r and at lines 30 and 40 we decide which half of the range it falls in. If it's less than .5 we print "heads", if it's greater than or equal to .5 we print "tails". It's as easy as that! We haven't really written an inspiring coin tossing program so we will return to this problem a little later on.

What if you had a crooked penny? One that said heads three-quarters of the time? It's not difficult to see how we would alter the program to give the results that the bad penny would give. Simply change the division of the range into two unequal parts. In general, if the probability of getting heads is p then:

```
10 RAND 0
20 INPUT p
30 LET r=RND
40 IF r<p THEN PRINT "heads"
50 IF r>=p THEN PRINT "tails"
60 GOTO 30
```

For tossing a coin, all we have to do is allow for two possibilities, each of which occur with the same probability — unless we deliberately alter the odds as in the bad penny example. There are other random situations where there are a larger number of possibilities and where the chances of the different outcomes are not equal to one another.

To the ordinary onlooker, the weather in this country often seems to be a matter of chance — or rather mischance. Let's write a program to see if the weathermen do get it right by forecasting using scientific principles, more often than if they just made an "educated guess". The guess combines a random element with our knowledge of seasonable weather patterns. The following program has been written for spring. In the 100 days of spring (the period from mid-February to mid-May) you might expect 40 sunny days, 30 cloudy days, 20 rainy days and 10 days of snowfall, putting this in terms of probability: sun on .40 of the days, cloud on .30 of the days, rain on .20 of the days and snow on .10 of them. Let's see how this fits together. Consider a line with 0 at one end and 1 at the other and mark off sections the same in length as the probability of each type of weather. For example:

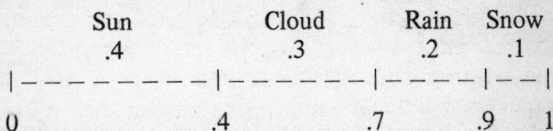

```
      Sun              Cloud          Rain   Snow
       .4                .3            .2      .1
 | — — — — — — — — | — — — — — — | — — — — | — — |

 0                   .4              .7      .9    1
```

If we produce random numbers evenly between 0 and 1 the probability of a number falling in any given section of the line is proportional to the length of that section. This is the key to selecting the weather with the correct probability. The weather condition corresponding to the section in which the random number occurs is the one predicted. So for the number .6712348117, "Cloud" is given.

There is a problem with this. What if the random number is exactly one of the borderline points, say .4; will it be sunny or cloudy? It's not that important which we chose as long as we decide. The correct choice is, in fact, to give the 0 point to the first section and carry on giving the boundary to the section to the right. What about the point corresponding to 1? Well if you look carefully at the definition of RND, you'll find that it gives numbers from 0 up to *but not including* 1. So the point corresponding to 1 need not concern us because it is never selected. The program for weather forecasting should now be obvious:

```
10 RAND 0
20 LET r=RND
30 PRINT "The Weather Forecast"
40 IF r<.4 THEN PRINT "Sun"
50 IF r>=.4 AND r<.7 THEN PRINT "Cloud"
60 IF r>=.7 AND r<.9 THEN PRINT "Rain"
70 IF r>=.9 THEN PRINT "Snow"
```

The only difficult part of this program is testing which section the random number falls in but this should be understandable if you refer to the line diagram above. There are lots of very tricky ways of carrying out the test, some of which save memory and some of which are faster, but the one used above is the easiest to understand and will work on any machine.

Random integers

Dividing up the interval between 0 and 1 is one way of selecting which "event" is going to happen. But it's not the only way. In a case where a given number of events occur with equal probability, there is an alternative — which is to multiply the number output by the computer by the number of possibilities, round it off to a whole number and add one to the answer. In fact this is easier than it sounds. Let's look at the practical example of throwing a dice. We have to choose one of 6 possibilities. We could use the method of dividing the line into 6 equal parts but instead let's try the new method. If we multiply RND by 6 we have a number that lies from 0 to less than 6. If we use the INT function to convert the number to an integer — a whole number — we have a number that lies between 0 and 5. Adding 1 gives a number between 1 and 6. To see this in action try the following program:

```
10 RAND 0
20 LET r=RND
30 PRINT r
40 LET r=r*6
50 PRINT r
60 LET r=INT(r)
70 PRINT r
80 LET r=r+1
90 PRINT r
```

If you run it a few times you should be able to see what's going on. Of course in practice you would carry out the whole procedure in one statement:

```
10 RAND 0
20 LET r=INT(RND*6)+1
30 PRINT r
40 GOTO 20
```

In general, if you want to produce random numbers between n and m use

```
10 LET r=INT(RND*(m−n+1))+n
```

Usually n is 1 and then this simplifies to

```
10 LET r=INT(RND*m)+1
```

if you put m=6 you get the dice program back again.

It is important to realise that this very easy method of producing random events *only* works if each of the events is equally likely.

Two improved programs

So far we have looked at randomness but we haven't really produced any complete games programs. The reason for this is that randomness is usually found as some part of a bigger program. Even so it is possible to do a better job with the two small programs that we examined earlier.

First let's have a look at the coin tossing program. One of

the things that's usually missing from a computer coin tossing program is the suspense. A coin is tossed ... it flies through the air ... it spins a bit ... will it be heads ... or tails ... finally it stops! A computer tossing simply prints "heads" or "tails" faster than you can blink! Let's try to slow down the selection part of the program to give it an element of suspense. Try:

```
10 DIM b$(2,5)
20 RAND 0
30 INPUT "Do you want to gamble y/n ?";a$
40 IF a$<>"y" THEN STOP
50 INK 0:PAPER 6:CLS
60 INPUT "heads or tails ? ";a$
70 PRINT "So you think it will be ";a$
80 LET r=INT(RND*15)+10
90 LET b$(1)="heads"
100 LET b$(2)="tails"
110 LET k=0
120 FOR i=1 TO r
130 LET k=NOT k
140 PRINT AT 5,0;b$(k+1)
150 FOR j=1 TO i
160 NEXT j
170 NEXT i
180 IF a$(1)=b$(k+1,1) THEN PRINT "You win"
190 IF a$(1)<>b$(k+1,1) THEN PRINT "You lose!! "
200 GOTO 30
```

The program works on a rather different principle to the simple coin tossing program. Lines 10, 90 and 100 set up a string array containing the words "heads" and "tails". The FOR loop starting at line 120 and ending at 170 prints one of the two words each time through. The statement at line 130 may puzzle some readers — NOT k simply changes k to 0 if it's 1, and 1 if it's 0. It is this "flipping" of k each time through the loop that causes heads and tails to be alternately printed out. If k=0 then line 140 prints "heads", if k=1 it

30

prints "tails". The random element is introduced in line 80 where r is the number of times that the loop is carried out. Obviously if r is odd, then the final result will be heads; if it's even then the result will be tails. The final touch of suspense is added by making the words "heads" and ' tails" alternate more and more slowly as time goes on by including a delay loop at lines 150 to 160.

This program is not easy to understand so don't worry too much if you cannot follow all of it. Some of the commands and techniques will be described in more detail later on.

Our second improved program is a dice program. The improvement is obvious – we print out the usual dice patterns of dots for each result. We can save some programming by noticing that the pattern for three dots is the same as printing the pattern for two and the pattern for one. Similarly the pattern for four is the same as the pattern for two with two extra dots! And so on with five (four plus one) and six (four plus two extra dots). The resulting program is:

```
10 RAND 0
20 LET r=INT(RND*6)+1
30 GOSUB r*100
40 INPUT a$
50 IF a$="s" THEN STOP
60 INK 2:PAPER 6:CLS
70 GOTO 20
100 PRINT AT 5,5;"*"
110 RETURN
200 PRINT AT 0,0;"*"
210 PRINT AT 10,10;"*"
220 RETURN
300 GOSUB 100
310 GOTO 200
400 PRINT AT 0,10;"*"
410 PRINT AT 10,0;"*"
420 GOTO 200
500 GOSUB 400
510 GOTO 100
```

```
600 PRINT AT 5,0;"*"
610 PRINT AT 5,10;"*"
620 GOTO 400
```

         *   *

                   *

            *   *

The only clever bit of the program is line 30 which selects
subroutine 100 if r is 1, subroutine 200 if r is 2 etc. To use the
program, press ENTER for each throw of the dice and press
"s" when you have finished using it.

The trouble with cards

So far we have used random numbers to select which of a
number of events would happen. It might seem that we could
use the same methods to write programs that play card games.
A deck of cards consists of four suits each of 13 cards. There
are many ways of using a computer to pick a card. One of the
easiest to understand is to simply generate two random
numbers, one between 1 and 4 to select the suit, and one
between 1 and 13 to select which card. The problem with this
method is that if you draw a card — the ace of spades say —
there is nothing to stop you from drawing it again! This sort
of drawing of cards is the same as drawing a card, noting its
value and putting it back in the deck — it is drawing with
replacement. The more usual way to draw cards is to deal
them out and this is drawing without replacement. You can
arrange for this sort of drawing to be programmed but it does
take a lot of time — usually too much for a program in BASIC.
   The second problem with cards is that anyone who is good
at card games will tell you that a lot of the fun comes from
working out odds and trying to remember the order in which

the cards were dealt. Shuffling is a very inefficient way of rearranging the cards in a deck and if the last time around one card followed another then after shuffling the chances are that it will still follow the same card. It is the use of this fact that makes a good card player. Imagine then a good player's reaction to playing against a computer — there are no cards and the random draw is far too good to allow associations between pairs of cards to remain.

The solution to both the drawing without replacement and the inefficient shuffling problem lies in the computer simulation of a deck of cards. For example, if you set up a string containing 52 different symbols — one for each card in each suit — then dealing could be carried out by printing each symbol in turn. Randomness could be ensured by the occasional simulated shuffle. For example, for one suit

```
10 LET a$=" AH 2H 3H 4H 5H 6H 7H 8H
   9H10H JH QH KH"
20 GOSUB 100
30 LET i=1
40 PRINT a$ (i TO i+2)
50 LET i=i+3
60 IF i=13*3+1 THEN STOP
70 GOTO 40
100 FOR i=1 TO 13
110 LET j=INT (RND*13)
120 LET b$=a$(j*3+1 TO j*3+3)
130 LET a$=a$ (1 TO j*3) + a$(j*3+4 TO )
140 LET a$=a$+b$
150 NEXT i
160 RETURN
```

The array at line 10 represents the suit of cards from AH — Ace of Hearts to KH — King of Hearts. Subroutine 100 carries out a simple shuffling by selecting a card at random and putting it at the end of the deck 13 times. Lines 30 to 70 print out each card in turn. Notice that this is slow and that it results in a not very good shuffle.

```
9H
10H
JH
QH
KH
3H
8H
7H
4H
6H
2H
5H
AH
```

If you want to, you can call the subroutine again for a more thorough shuffle — insert

25 GOSUB 100

As you can see, shuffling alone requires a fairly complicated routine. However, if you're not too worried about shuffling it is possible to program a simple card game such as pontoon.

Pontoon

```
10 LET t=0
20 LET u=0
30 INK 6:PAPER 1:CLS
40 REM plays a hand
50 GOSUB 400
60 LET t=t+c
70 IF t>21 THEN GOTO 300
80 PRINT "You have ";t
90 PRINT "Stick or Twist s/t"
100 INPUT a$
110 IF a$="s" THEN GOTO 200
120 PRINT "Next card is - ";
130 GOTO 40
200 PRINT "Spectrum's turn to beat - "
210 PRINT "Your total of ";t
220 LET a$="Spectrum "
230 GOSUB 400
```

```
240 LET u=u+c
250 IF u>21 THEN GOTO 300
260 PRINT "Spectrum's total ";u
270 PAUSE 100
280 IF u<t THEN GOTO 230
290 PRINT FLASH 1;"Spectrum wins":GOTO 330
300 IF t>21 THEN PRINT"You are ";
310 IF u>21 THEN PRINT"Spectrum is ";
320 PRINT "BUST"
330 INPUT "For another hand press ENTER";a$
340 GOTO 10
400 REM picks a card
410 LET c=INT(RND*13)+1
420 LET a$=" "+STR$(c)
430 IF c=1 THEN LET a$="ACE"
440 IF c=11 THEN LET a$="JACK"
450 IF c=12 THEN LET a$="QUEEN"
460 IF c=13 THEN LET a$="KING"
470 PRINT a$
480 RETURN
```

```
         2
You have 2
Stick or Twist s/t
Next card is -   5
You have 7
Stick or Twist s/t
Next card is -   3
You have 10
Stick or Twist s/t
Next card is -   10
You have 20
Stick or Twist s/t

Spectrum's turn to beat -
Your total of 20
KING
Spectrum's total 13
  8
Spectrum's total 21
Spectrum wins
```

This is a simplified version of pontoon to make the principles behind the program easier to see. The card values are

ACE=1, JACK=11, QUEEN=12 and KING=13. The cards are drawn without replacement and without any reference to suit by line 410. The number is converted to a string by line 420 so that the cards can either be numbers, i.e. 2, 3, 4 etc. or words, i.e. ACE, KING etc.

Unequal probabilities — an advanced method

We can use a special feature of the Spectrum to generate a number corresponding to the interval into which a random number falls in the case of unequal sized intervals as well as equal sized ones. As we found earlier, if we want to generate four things with equal probability we can use

```
10 LET r=INT(RND*4)+1
```

but this will not work for unequal probabilities such as those used in the weather program. However:

```
10 LET r=RND
20 LET w= (r>.4) + (r>.7) + (r>.9) +1
30 PRINT w
40 GOTO 10
```

will produce numbers from 1 to 4 within the same (unequal) probabilities as the different weather conditions. It works because the Spectrum "works out" if tests such as r<.4 are true or false and uses 1 to mean true and 0 to mean false. To understand line 20 let's suppose that r is .5; r is bigger than .4 so the first bracket works out to be 1 but r is smaller in all the other tests so the second and third brackets work out to be 0. When you add together all the 1s and 0s — with the extra 1 — you get the answer that w is 2. If you try it for other values of r you can convince yourself that w is the number of the intervals that r falls in (starting at 1).

You could use this method to make the dice or coin tossing program given earlier unfair. But we leave this as a project for you to try for yourself!

Randomness and symmetry

No doubt you have seen the fascinating displays of continuously changing patterns that other computers produce. Well, the Spectrum can do the same sort of thing.

Let's start with a truly random pattern

```
10 LET x=INT(RND*32)
20 LET y=INT(RND*22)
30 LET c=INT(RND*8)
40 PRINT AT y,x;INK c;"[^8]";
50 GOTO 10
```

(Notice the use of the graphics notation introduced in Chapter Two in line 40.) Lines 10 and 20 generate random positions to print the graphics character at and line 30 selects an ink colour at random. The results of this program are interesting but hardly the type of pattern that you could watch for long. The trouble is that the pattern is too random. Interesting and ever changing patterns must use randomness for variety but they must use it in a controlled way. One of the basic organising principles in nature is symmetry and this can be used in computer patterns to introduce order.

In Spectrum BASIC it is fairly easy to handle four-fold symmetry and this is quite powerful enough to produce many interesting patterns. Four-fold symmetry is best understood by thinking of the Spectrum's screen split into four quarters. If a character is printed in the first quarter then a symmetrical pattern will be produced if it is also printed in the other three regions. If you imagine that the two lines that divide the screen into four quarters are mirrors then the position of the other three points can be thought of as mirror images of the original. If the co-ordinate of the original point in the first quarter is X,Y then the co-ordinates of the mirror images are $31-X,Y$; $X,21-Y$ and $31-X,21-Y$. The best way to see that this is true is to use a piece of graph paper to draw the screen and work out the co-ordinates. Using these simple facts we can write a kaleidoscope program:

```
10 LET m=31
20 LET n=21
30 LET x=RND*m/2
40 LET y=RND*n/2
50 LET c=INT(RND*8)
60 INK c
70 PRINT AT y,x;"[^8]";
80 PRINT AT y,m-x;"[^8]";
90 PRINT AT n-y,x;"[^8]";
100 PRINT AT n-y,m-x;"[^8]";
110 GOTO 30
```

Lines 30 and 40 generate the position of the graphics block and line 50 generates an ink colour. Line 60 sets the ink colour for all the following PRINT statements in lines 70 to 100.

Using this basic idea of four-fold symmetry it is possible to add other controlling features to make interesting patterns. It might be interesting if the random changes went in "cyles" starting at the middle and working out. You can see this idea in practice below:

```
10 LET m=31
20 LET n=21
```

```
   30 FOR x=0 TO m/2
   40 LET y=RND*n/2 -10
 * 50 LET c=INT(RND*8); INK c
   60 PRINT AT-y,x;"[^8]";          ⌐
   70 PRINT AT-y,m-x;"[^8]";        ⌐
   80 PRINT AT-n-y,x;"[^8]";        ⌐
   90 PRINT AT-n-y,m-x;"[^8]";      ⌐
   100 NEXT x
   110 GOTO 30
```

The result of this program is difficult to capture in print because it depends on movement, but a typical output (which would be in colour of course) might look like this:

Randomness and symmetry can be used to produce patterns other than the usual "spotty" sort. If we start off with a point in the center of the screen and let it wander around randomly by adding −1,0 or 1 to each of its co-ordinates we have a fairly interesting random line. But if we also use the four-fold symmetry routine to reflect the line into each quarter, the result is a collection of fascinating shapes:

39

```
10 LET m=31
20 LET n=21
30 LET x=m/2
40 LET y=n/2
50 GOSUB 100
60 LET x=x+RND*2-1
70 LET y=y+RND*2-1
80 GOTO 50
100 PRINT AT y,x;"[^8]";
110 PRINT AT y,m-x;"[^8]";
120 PRINT AT n-y,x;"[^8]";
130 PRINT AT n-y,m-x;"[^8]";
140 RETURN
```

We could continue for a lot longer with random patterns but we'll leave the rest of the subject for you to explore for yourselves.

40

Chapter Four

HIGH RESOLUTION GRAPHICS

Chapter Two introduced the idea behind Spectrum graphics and described the two types of dot — ink and paper — that make up the display. By printing characters and graphics shapes in the character locations on the screen, it is possible to create impressive and finely detailed graphics. However, if you want to draw graphs or outline figures then you need to be able to change dots on the screen in a way that ignores character locations — this is the realm of high resolution graphics. The PLOT command can change any dot from ink to paper or vice versa without affecting any other and DRAW can produce straight and curved lines anywhere on the screen. Perhaps the most advanced high resolution graphics command is CIRCLE which, not surprisingly, can be used to draw a circle of a given radius. For a machine as reasonably priced as the Spectrum this high resolution capability is very impressive. However, if you want to produce high resolution graphics in full colour then there are some problems.

Specifying a point

Obviously if you are going to use commands that alter individual dots on the screen you must have some way of specifying which dot. This is easily solved by the usual trick of stating the row and column number of the dot in question. The column number is usually referred to as the "x co-ordinate" and the row number is usually referred to as the "y co-ordinate". The rows and columns numbers all start from zero and, as the Spectrum's screen is a rectangle composed of 256 dots horizontally and 176 dots vertically, this means that the x co-ordinate varies from 0 to 255 and the y co-ordinate varies from 0 to 175. The only extra complication is that the y co-ordinate starts at zero at the *bottom* of the screen. This is of course the opposite way round to the line number used in a

PRINT AT statement. In other words, in high resolution graphics the point with x co-ordinate zero and y co-ordinate zero is in the *bottom* left hand corner.

The high resolution graphics commands

Before going on to consider how high resolution graphics can be used in programs, it is worth looking at the three high resolution commands in detail. The basic high resolution command is.

PLOT x,y

changes the dot at x,y into an ink dot. Both x and y can be arithmetic expressions. In fact the only restriction is that x and y are valid screen co-ordinates. In other words, x has to be in the range 0 to 255 and y in the range 0 to 175, any other values cause an error message to be printed. To see the PLOT command in action try:

```
10 INPUT x,y
20 PLOT x,y
30 GOTO 10
```

To fill the screen with ink dots try:

```
10 FOR x=0 TO 255
20 FOR y=0 TO 175
30 PLOT x,y
40 NEXT y
50 NEXT x
```

Notice that so far we can only use PLOT to produce ink dots, how to produce paper dots will be discussed after all of the high resolution graphics commands have been introduced.

The DRAW command is used in conjunction with the PLOT command to produce lines. The statement

DRAW x,y

will draw a line starting at the place where the last point was plotted. The finishing point of the line is x points horizontally and y points vertically away from the start. The fact that the

42

starting point of the line depends on a previous command and the finishing point isn't given explicitly makes DRAW seem a difficult command to use. However, in practice it fits in very well with the way high resolution graphics tend to be used. The combined command

PLOT x,y:DRAW xd,yd

draws a line between the point x,y and x+xd,y+yd. Some simple arithmetic shows that

PLOT x1,y1:DRAW x2-x1,y2-y1

will draw a line between x1,y1 and x2,y2. To investigate the DRAW command a little more try the following

10 PLOT 100,50
20 DRAW 25,25

This plots a point at 100,50 and then draws a diagonal line "upwards and to the right". However,

10 PLOT 100,50
20 DRAW -25,-25

also draws a diagonal line starting from the same point but the line now goes "down and to the left". This last example highlights an important difference between PLOT and DRAW. While negative numbers don't make any sense when used with PLOT if you want to draw lines from the top of the screen to the bottom or from right to left then you have to use negative numbers.

You might be wondering what happens if you follow one DRAW command immediately by another. Where does the second line start from? The answer is that it starts from the final point produced by the first DRAW command. A useful way of thinking about this is to imagine an invisible "graphics cursor" that moves about the screen as points are plotted. Thus after any command, the cursor is positioned at the last point plotted. The DRAW command always starts drawing a line from the current cursor position. You can use a number of DRAW commands one after the other to produce continuous outlines. For example to draw a square

```
10 PLOT 50,100
20 DRAW 50,0
30 DRAW 0,-50
40 DRAW -50,0
50 DRAW 0,50
```

The first command can be thought of as moving the graphics cursor to 50,100 and the DRAW commands produce the sides of the square and move the cursor for the next DRAW command.

The final high resolution command is

CIRCLE x,y,r

which will draw the best approximation to a circle that the Spectrum can manage on its 256 by 176 grid of points. The circle will be centered on the point x,y and have a radius determined by r. As a demonstration of CIRCLE try:

```
10 FOR r=0 TO 80 STEP 2
20 CIRCLE 128,80,r
30 NEXT r
```

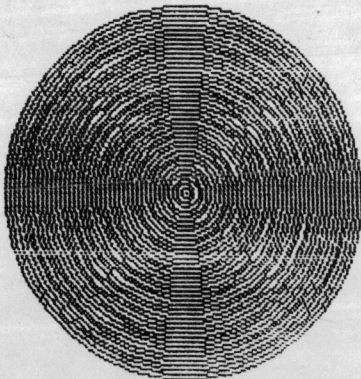

This program produces an interesting pattern by plotting a number of circles all centered on 120,80. The CIRCLE command is relatively easy to use, in fact the only thing that you have to be careful of is going off the screen. We will return to the subject of circles later in this chapter.

INVERSE, OVER and attributes

The high resolution graphics commands can be used in conjunction with the commands INVERSE, OVER and the attribute commands INK, PAPER, FLASH and BRIGHT. It is not difficult to work out the effects that these commands have as long as you remember that attributes can only be set for whole character locations and not for individual points. You can even place such commands within high resolution graphics commands in the same way that they can be included in PRINT statements. However, their effect can be rather unexpected as we shall see. It is easier to consider the two commands INVERSE and OVER before the attribute commands.

If you plot a point following INVERSE 1 then instead of an ink dot you will produce a paper dot. This is true for all the graphics commands so if you have just produced a circle of ink dots using the CIRCLE command you can remove it, i.e. change it back to paper dots, by

CIRCLE INVERSE 1,x,y,r

In other words, PLOT INVERSE 1,x,y can be thought of as "unplotting" or removing a point. One thing to be careful of when using INVERSE to remove lines that have been plotted using DRAW is that you specify exactly the same line the second time. For example, if you produce a line by

10 PLOT 10,10:DRAW 100,100

then you must use

10 PLOT 10,10:DRAW INVERSE 1,100,100

and not

10 PLOT 100,100:DRAW INVERSE 1,-100,-100

which attempts to remove the line but starting at the original lines finishing point. To be certain of removing every point you must always unplot in the same direction.

You can also use OVER with high resolution graphics. However, as the high resolution commands normally only produce ink dots its action is comparatively simple. If there is already an ink dot present at the location then a high resolution graphics command that tries to produce an ink dot will actually result in a paper dot. If instead there is a paper dot present then a high resolution graphics command will produce an ink dot. In other words, following an OVER 1 high resolution graphics commands change existing ink dots to paper and existing paper dots to ink.

If you combine OVER 1 with INVERSE 1 then the two effects cancel out. INVERSE 1 makes all the high resolution commands produce paper dots but, by the rules of OVER 1 (see Chapter Two), a paper dot plotted at the same location as an existing ink dot produces an ink dot. As a paper dot plotted at the same location as an existing paper dot produces a paper dot you should be able to see that this leaves everything unchanged. This doesn't mean that

PLOT INVERSE 1,OVER 1,x,y

is useless as if it doesn't alter any dots on the screen. It can be used to move the graphics cursor without plotting anything.

The subject of attributes and high resolution graphics is slightly more complicated than INVERSE and OVER because attributes are defined over complete character locations rather than single points. So while you can use the commands INK, PAPER, BRIGHT and FLASH with high resolution commands and you can even include them within such commands they affect the whole character location that a point falls in. The result of this is that if you plot a green ink dot then all the other ink dots in the character location that the point falls in will also change to green. The same is true for plotting paper dots, flashing dots and bright dots. In other words, whatever attributes you give to a single dot these attributes are immediately shared by all the other dots within the same character location. To see this in action try:

10 PLOT INK 3,10,10

```
20 DRAW INK 3,100,100
30 PLOT INK 5,10,100
40 DRAW INK 5,PAPER 2,100,-100
```

The first two statements draw a red diagonal line. Lines 30
and 40 draw a diagonal line that crosses the first. There are
two things to notice about the results of this program. Firstly,
where the two lines cross in a single character location there
can only be ONE ink colour and this is the colour of the last
line to be plotted, i.e. ink 5, cyan. Secondly, and more surprisingly, the PAPER command in line 40 affects each of the
character locations that the line passes through even though
the DRAW command produces only ink dots! This should be
considered as a warning to take care when using attributes
in high resolution commands.

In practical terms, what this restriction on attributes and
colours in particular means is that high resolution graphics is
easier to use in two colours only. If you want to use the full
range of Spectrum colours then you will need to plan your
displays so that no more than two colours meet in any
character location. This is often impossible unless you are
dealing with very simple shapes. However, only using two
colours in high resolution graphics is not too unsatisfactory for
many of the tasks that high resolution graphics are best suited
to, for example, plotting graphs.

Circles and ellipses

Although the Spectrum has a command that will produce very
good circles very quickly, it is still worth knowing how to
produce a circle from first principles. Also once you know
how to draw a circle you can soon discover how to draw an
elipse and if you don't know why you might want to draw an
elipse then see the "baked bean tin" later in this section!

The co-ordinates of any point on a circle centred at x1,y1
and radius r satisfy the following two equations:

$$x=r*SIN(t)+x1$$

and

$$y = r*COS(t) + y1$$

for some value of t. It doesn't matter if you don't understand these equations you can still make use of them. The important point is that if you give t any value and work out the two equations you have a point on the circle. Try the following:

```
10 LET r=60
20 LET x1=100
30 LET y1=60
40 LET t=RND*6.283
50 PLOT r*SIN(t)+x1,r*COS(t)+y1
60 GOTO 40
```

You should see a circle appear on the screen in random order. We have used RND to produce random values of t and hence random points on the circle. If we want to, we can start with t=0 and, by increasing t slowly plot all the points on the circle. It just so happens that the circle joins up with itself when t reaches the odd value 6.283 and this just happens to be twice the value of π. (There is a very good mathematical reason for this but it need not worry us.) We can use the PI key on the Spectrum instead of the rough approximation:

```
10 LET r=60
20 FOR t=0 TO 2*PI STEP .01
30 PLOT r*SIN t +100,r*COS t +80
40 NEXT t
```

If you run the above program you will see a circle appear but much more slowly than one produced by the CIRCLE command. Try experimenting with different values of the step size to produce circles of different "roughness".

The circles produced using SIN and COS should, in theory at least, be as accurate as the limited resolution of the Spectrum's 256-by-176 screen allows. The method by which CIRCLE draws circles is not explained anywhere in the Spectrum Manual and there is no guarantee that the circles are totally accurate. It is interesting to compare the two methods. The following program first draws a circle using the SIN/COS

48

formula and then draws the same circle using CIRCLE. The points where both circles coincide are returned to paper dots because of the OVER 1 command at line 50. Thus, the only points that are left as ink at the end of the program are where the two methods produce different circles.

```
10 LET r=60
20 FOR t=0 TO 2*PI STEP .01
30 PLOT r*SIN t +100,r*COS t +80
40 NEXT t
50 OVER 1
60 CIRCLE 100,80,60
```

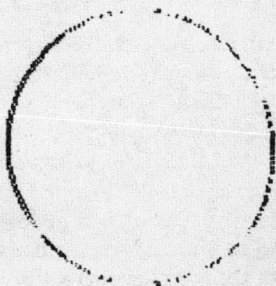

Although the two methods do produce slightly different circles they are not very different and considering the speed of CIRCLE the inaccuracy is forgiveable.

Knowing the co-ordinates of points that lie on a circle can have other uses than just simply drawing circles! For example, if you draw lines from the centre to the circumference you can make some interesting patterns. Try:

```
10 LET r=80
20 LET c=INT(RND*8)
30 INK c
40 PAPER 9
50 CLS
60 FOR t=0 TO 2*PI STEP (RND+RND)/10
70 LET x=r*SIN t
```

```
80 LET y=r*COS t
90 PLOT 128,80
100 DRAW x,y
110 NEXT t
120 PAUSE 100
130 GOTO 20
```

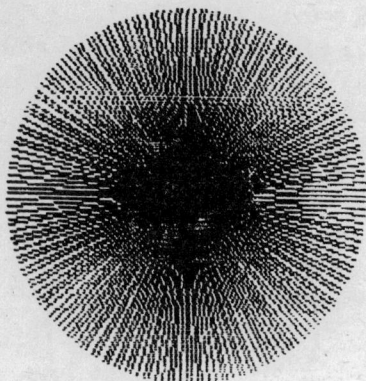

Line 90 moves the graphics cursor to the center of the circle and line 100 draws a line to the circumference. Notice the use of colour 9 to produce a contrasting background to the pattern.

Once you know how to produce circles it is not difficult to extend the method to produce ellipses. As you probably already know an ellipse is a sort of "flattened" circle. It's what you see when you view a circle at an oblique angle and so is very useful if you want to produce any three dimensional drawings of circular objects. To draw an ellipse you can use the same formula as circle but with two values for the radius — a horizontal radius and a vertical radius. Try the following:

```
10 LET r1=100
20 LET r2=40
30 FOR t=0 TO 2*PI STEP .01
40 PLOT r1*SIN t +128,r2*COS t +80
50 NEXT t
```

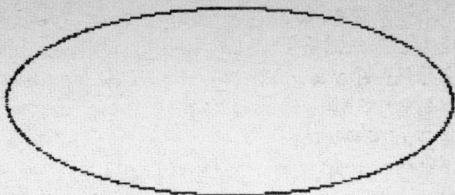

which draws an ellipse with a horizontal radius of 100 and a vertical radius of 40. Try other values of r1 and r2 to produce different shaped ellipses.

As an example of using ellipses to draw a three dimensional object try the following "tin can" program:

```
10 FOR t=0 TO 2*PI STEP .02
20 PLOT 50*SIN t+128,10*COS t+100
25 PLOT 50*SIN t+128,10*COS t+20
30 NEXT t
40 PLOT 128+50,20
50 DRAW 0,80
60 PLOT 128-50,20
70 DRAW 0,80
```

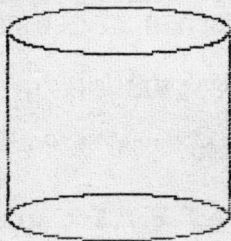

You should be able to find the two ellipses in this program!

Arrows game

The arrows game is a simple application of high resolution graphics. Two arrows each of random length are drawn. The length of the second arrow can be adjusted by pressing the "left arrow" key which makes it shorter or by pressing the "right arrow" key which makes it longer. The object of the game is to make the second arrow the same length as the first. This sounds easy until you try it — there is a well known optical illusion at work!

```
10 LET L=INT((RND*20)+140)
20 PLOT 50,120
30 DRAW L,0
40 PLOT 50,120
50 DRAW -25,25
60 PLOT 50,120
70 DRAW -25,-25
80 PLOT 50+L,120
90 DRAW 25,25
100 PLOT 50+L,120
110 DRAW 25,-25
120 LET s=INT((RND*50)+100)
130 GOSUB 500
140 LET a$=INKEY$
150 IF a$="" THEN GOTO 140
160 IF a$="s" THEN GOTO 300
170 IF a$="5" THEN GOSUB 500:LET s=s-1:
    GOTO 130
180 IF a$="8" THEN GOSUB 500:LET s=s+1:
    GOTO 130
190 GOTO 140

300 PRINT AT 18,0;"Top arrow=";L
310 PRINT AT 19,0;"Bottom=";s
320 PRINT AT 20,0;"Which is a difference of"
330 PLOT 50,4
340 DRAW ABS(L-s),0
350 IF L=s THEN PLOT OVER 1;50,4
360 STOP

500 OVER 1
```

```
510 PLOT 50,50
520 DRAW s,0
530 PLOT 50,50
540 DRAW 25,25
550 PLOT 50,50
560 DRAW 25,-25
570 PLOT 50+s,50
580 DRAW -25,-25
590 PLOT 50+s,50
600 DRAW -25,25
610 OVER 0
620 RETURN
```

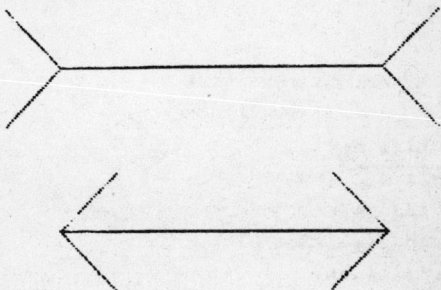

Lines 10 to 110 draw the first arrow on the screen. Line 120 selects a random length for the second arrow and this is drawn by subroutine 500.Notice the use of OVER in subroutine 500. The first call to subroutine 500 produces the arrow on the screen and a second call with the same length removes it from the screen. Lines 140 to 180 test to see which key is being pressed, if any. A right-arrow key increases the length of the line and replots the arrow and a left-arrow key reduces the length of the line and replots it. If you press the s key then lines 300 to 350 print the actual lengths of the arrows and draw the difference in the form of a short line.

Although this is quite a simple program when you use it, it does give the impression that the second arrow actually moves in response to which key you are pressing.

Too much resolution

One mistake that is often made by beginners is the over-use of high resolution graphics. It has already been stated that many things are easier and better done in low resolution graphics. As an example consider the random symmetry programs discussed in Chapter Two. If you were thinking about writing a program of this type from scratch then you might be tempted to use high resolution graphics in an attempt to produce a more complicated pattern. The first result of this approach is that the pattern can only be created in two colours — whereas the low resolution version of the program can use all eight colours. Even if you accept this restriction to two colours and proceed with the high resolution program you might feel a little disappointed with the overall effect. Try:

```
10 OVER 1
20 LET x=INT(RND*128)
30 LET y=INT(RND*88)
40 PLOT x,y
50 PLOT 255-x,y
60 PLOT x,175-y
70 PLOT 255-x,175-y
80 GOTO 20
```

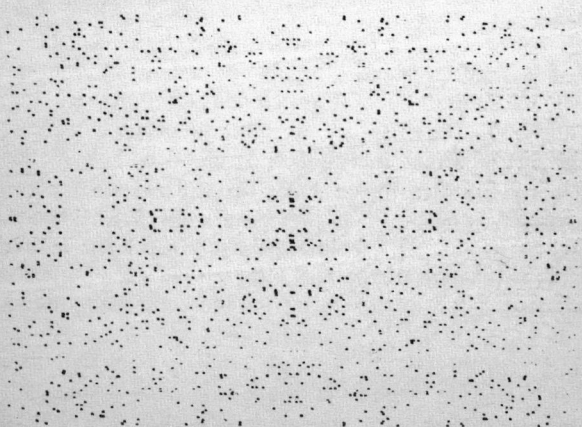

It is true that this program does produce a complex pattern but for many people it is too complex to be interesting. The dots are too small — the resolution is too high!

An advanced form of DRAW

This section discusses a slightly more advanced form of the DRAW command and may be skipped on first reading. The full form of the DRAW command is

DRAW x,y,t

where x and y have the same meaning as before and t is an angle measured in radians. The best way to explain what the new form of DRAW does is by example:

10 PLOT x1,y1:DRAW x2-x1,y2-y1

draws a straight line between the points x1,y1 and x2,y2. The command,

10 PLOT x1,y1:DRAW x2-x1,y2-y1,t

also draws a line between x1,y1 and x2,y2 but instead of a straight line it uses a portion of a circle. The size of the portion is governed by the value of t. If you are not familiar with measuring angles in radians you will find the following table useful:

t	part of a circle
2*PI	whole
PI	half
PI/2	quarter

The trouble with the extended version of DRAW is that it is difficult to ensure that the curve drawn remains on the screen for its entire length. However, if you need to draw part of a circle then DRAW is the best way. For example, to draw a semi circle:

10 PLOT 100,80
20 DRAW 50,50,PI/2

There are two ways to draw a circular arc between two points

— clockwise or anit-clockwise. To see how to draw the other arc in the above example change the PI/2 to —PI/2.

The extended DRAW command is not used very often simply because drawing parts of circles is not something that crops up a great deal.

Chapter Five

SOUND

The ability to make sounds through its own tiny internal loud-speaker is a feature of the Spectrum that can be used to bring a new excitement to games. Also, if you've always been interested in music but have lacked either the patience, time or skill to learn to play a musical instrument, then the Spectrum is an ideal way to find out about the subject. There are a number of problems with sound on the Spectrum however; it can only produce one note at a time, you cannot control the volume of a note nor its quality, sound effects are difficult to get at from BASIC and finally, unlike some more expensive machines, the Spectrum can only do one thing at a time — either make noises or run programs. The result of this last problem is that if you want to play a game with a musical accompaniment then you will find it difficult to do from BASIC. It is possible to overcome some of these problems by clever programming but if after reading this chapter you become completely hooked on computer music, you will either have to move to the more difficult area of writing machine code programs or improve on your Spectrum. However before you have to take such drastic steps there is a lot to learn and a lot of fun to be had from Spectrum sounds using nothing other than BASIC.

BEEP and PAUSE

The only sound command that the Spectrum has is BEEP:

BEEP duration,pitch

which sounds the loudspeaker for a particular duration at the specified pitch. The "duration" can be any valid expression and is measured in seconds. The "pitch" can also be any valid expression but it's measured in a slightly more complicated way as semitones above and below middle C (this will be explained in more detail later on). The most important thing to realise about the BEEP command is that it takes "duration" seconds to complete. This means that if you produce a sound for ten seconds, say, you cannot expect your Spectrum to do anything else for that time. This makes BEEP rather like a PAUSE but with sound! In contrast, some computers provide sound commands that start a sound off and then the program continues by executing the next instruction almost immediately. This is obviously a much more satisfactory situation and later in this chapter we will explore how to get a similar effect from the Spectrum.

The BEEP command provides a way of sounding a note for a given length of time but in many applications, playing music for example, it is also important to be able to produce a silence for a given length of time. This can easily be achieved on the Spectrum by using the PAUSE command,

PAUSE duration

which will simply cause the machine to wait around doing absolutely nothing for a period of time. There are two things to be careful of, however, when using the PAUSE command in conjunction with the BEEP command. The first is simply that the PAUSE "duration" is measured in fiftieths of a second (sixtieths of a second in the USA and some other places) as it depends on the TV frame rate — see Chapter Eight for more details. The easiest way around this problem is to write all PAUSE commands as

PAUSE duration*50

which will convert "duration" in seconds to fiftieths of a second automatically. The second problem is that a PAUSE can be cut short by pressing any key on the keyboard and there is no real remedy for this apart from being aware of it and keeping fingers away from the keyboard during music with pauses!

The way that the Spectrum actually produces sound is very simple. As you probably already know, sound is vibrations in the air and the Spectrum produces such vibrations by moving the cone of its tiny loudspeaker in and out. The frequency of the sound produced depends on the number of times per second the loudspeaker cone moves in and out and this is really the only control you have over the Spectrum's sound. There are only two states that the cone can be in — fully out or fully in. One movement from fully in to fully out and back produces a click. If you want to hear this click try:

BEEP .001,0

If this movement is repeated you will begin to hear a continuous sound instead of a single click and as the number of clicks per second increases so the pitch or frequency of the note increases. To hear this try:

```
10 FOR i=-60 TO 69
20 BEEP .5,i
30 NEXT i
```

This example also indicates the range of notes that you can produce. In practice the range of useful notes is much smaller than this because the very high notes sound uneven and the low notes very quickly become rasping.

Playing written music

Playing a tune is easy! It's all a matter of producing the correct pitch at the correct time and for the correct duration. The only trouble is that music has been around for a lot longer than the digital computer and musicians have invented their own form of programming language — musical notation. Fortunately musical notation is not too difficult to understand and it is possible for anyone to learn to read music in a very short time.

Musical notation conveys two pieces of information — what pitch a sound should have and how long it should last for. The pitch of a note is indicated by its position on a row of lines known as a musical stave. Every note is named according to which line it falls on as shown in Fig 1.

Fig. 1   Musical stave and note names

Starting from middle C the note names go alphabetically to G and then start again with A then B and back to C. The occurrence of C more than once is no accident and corresponds to the fact that we actually hear notes with the same name as sounding the same. The musical distance between any two notes with the same name is called an "octave".

The only problem is in converting these note names into "pitch" values for the Spectrum. The line marked middle C corresponds to a pitch value of zero and increasing the pitch value by one takes us up one "semitone" subtracting one from the pitch value takes us down by the same amount. So if we start at middle C with a pitch value of zero, it sounds as though if we want to go up a whole note to D we should add 2, and indeed this is correct. If 1 corresponds to a semitone then 2 corresponds to a whole tone. The next step is to say that going from D to E would be accomplished by adding 2 to the pitch value which is also correct but adding 2 to E does *not* take us to the note F! The fact of the matter is that, in Western music at least, there isn't always a whole tone between two named notes. This is also revealed by examining a standard piano keyboard. The familiar pattern of black and white keys indicates how "far apart" each pair of notes are starting at middle C the pattern is

```
   T T S T T T S
   C D E F G A B C
```

Thus going from E to F only requires the Spectrum's pitch value to increase by 1.

If all this seems a little over-complicated and you think that musical notes really all have the same semitone "distance" between them try the following two short programs:

```
10 FOR i=0 TO 14 STEP 2
20 BEEP .5,i
30 NEXT i
```

and

```
10 DATA 0,2,4,5,7,9,11,12
20 FOR i=1 TO 8
30 READ p
40 BEEP .5,p
50 NEXT i
```

The first program plays a "scale" assuming that there is a whole tone between each note and the second program plays the (correct) scale of C. You should prefer the scale produced by the second program and even if you don't this is the one most people prefer! The second program also introduces the idea of a data statement holding the pitch values to be played by the Spectrum — an idea that we will use again and again. Using this pattern of tone/semitone "distances" we arrive at the following correspondence between the different stave lines and pitch values.

C	D	E	F	G	A	B	C	D	E	F
0	2	4	5	7	9	11	12	14	16	17

Fig. 2 Stave lines and pitch values

All you have to do to convert a piece of written music into pitch values is to use the correspondence given in Fig. 2. The only extra complication is that musicians sometimes want to make a note higher or lower in pitch than its name would make it. To do this the "sharp" # and "flat" ♭ symbols are used to indicate the rising of a pitch by a semitone and the lowering of a pitch by a semitone. So whenever you see either a sharp

61

or flat symbol just work out the pitch value for the note as normal and then add or subtract 1 to sharpen or flatten it as required. There are two ways that sharps and flats can be indicated — by writing the symbols next to particular notes or in the "key signature" at the beginning of each stave. If the symbols occur at the beginning of the music then the sharpening and flattening effect applies to *all* the notes in that position throughout the piece of music. Not only does this apply to notes falling in the same position on the ledger lines as the sharp or flat symbol it also applies to all the notes with the same name. That is, a sharpening or flattening of a note that is written at the start of the music applies to that *note* and its *octaves* all the way through the music. However, if a sharp or flat symbol is written next to a particular note in the body of the music then the sharpening and flattening effect applies to only that note.

The second aspect of musical notation — the duration of each note — is easier to understand. Each note is assumed to last for some multiple of a basic unit of time. If we assume that a "normal" note — a crochet — lasts for one time unit then each oblique tail drawn on the note halves the time that the note lasts — see Fig. 3. There·are also notes that last longer than the crotchet, starting with the minim and the semibreve. which last for two and four time units respectively. If you look at some real music you will find that some notes are grouped together by joining the tails between them. These and other so-called phrasing and accent marks have no real importance when translating music to the Spectrum because it cannot vary the volume of the note it produces. The only other thing that you need to know about the duration of notes apart from the information contained in Fig. 3, is that a dot '.' following a note increases its length by half its natural duration. For example, a crotchet followed by a dot should last for $1\frac{1}{2}$ time units. A rest or a pause in the music is indicated by the use of the symbols shown in Fig. 3.

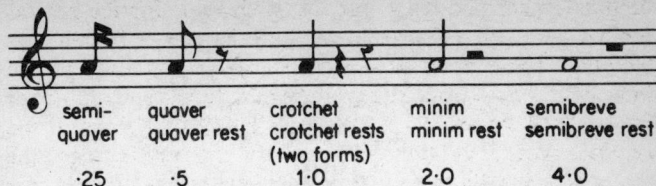

	semi- quaver	quaver quaver rest	crotchet crotchet rests (two forms)	minim minim rest	semibreve semibreve rest
	·25	·5	1·0	2·0	4·0

Fig. 3   Lengths of notes and rests

The Spectrum plays a tune

After all this theory about musical notation an example is
due. The first few bars of the familiar traditional American
tune "Dixie" can be seen in Fig. 4.

Names	F	D	B		B		B	C	D	E	F		F		F		D
Pitch	5	2	-2		-2		-2	0	2	3	5		5		5		2
Duration	$\frac{1}{4}$	$\frac{1}{4}$	$\frac{1}{2}$		$\frac{1}{2}$		$\frac{1}{4}$	$\frac{1}{4}$	$\frac{1}{4}$	$\frac{1}{4}$	$\frac{1}{2}$		$\frac{1}{2}$		$\frac{1}{2}$		$\frac{1}{2}$

Fig. 4   Dixie

The first job is to write the names of the notes under each one.
Then convert these note names to pitch values remembering
to take into account the flats at the start of the music. Finally
the durations, as fractions of the unit time interval are written
down.

After all this coding all that is left is to write the program.
There are many ways in which this could be done but perhaps
one of the most versatile is to use a DATA statement. Each
pair of numbers — pitch and duration — is written into a
DATA statement and the end of the music is indicated by
some pair of values such as 99,99 which are nonsense as pitch
and duration values. The complete program including the rest
of "Dixie" is:

```
10 DATA 5,.25,2,.25,-2,.5,-2,.5,-2,.25
20 DATA 0,.25,2,.25,3,.25,5,.5,5,.5,5,.5
30 DATA 2,.5,7,.5,7,.5,7,.5,5,.5,7,.5
40 DATA 7,.5,7,.25,9,.5,10,.25,12,.25
50 DATA 14,1.5,10,.25,5,.25,10,1.5,5,.25
60 DATA 14,.25,5,1.5,12,.25,14,.25,10,1.5
70 DATA 5,.25,5,.25,10,.5,14,.5,12,.5
80 DATA 10,.5,7,.5,10,1,10,.5,12,1.5,7,.5
90 DATA 12,1.5,5,.5,10,.5,14,.5,12,.5,10,.5
100 DATA 7,.5,9,.5,10,.75,7,.25,7,.25
110 DATA 5,.5,10,.5,2,.5,2,.5,0,1,2,.5
120 DATA -2,.75 2,.5,0,.75,7,.5,5,.5,2,.5
130 DATA 10,.75,14,.25,12,.5,10,1,99,99
140 LET d=.5
150 READ p,t
160 IF p=99 THEN STOP
170 BEEP d*t,p
180 GOTO 150
```

The technique for programming other tunes is the same. If a pause is required this can be coded as a nonsense pitch value followed by the time required for the pause.

Playing music

The other side of the coin from programming the Spectrum to play music, is to write a program that turns it into a musical instrument. You could then use your Spectrum to play existing music or even compose your own. The basic idea is easy to implement. You can use the INKEY$ function to read the keyboard to see if any key is pressed. If it is then all you have to do is to produce the pitch that you want the key to correspond to. Herein lies the difficulty — assigning the various pitches, tones and semitones to a keyboard with a typewriter keyboard is very difficult to do in a way that results in an easy to play "instrument". However as an example of such a program try the following

```
10 DATA 0,2,4,5,7,9,11,12
20 DIM n(8)
30 FOR i=1 TO 8
40 READ n(i)
50 NEXT i
60 LET a$=INKEY$
70 IF a$="" THEN GOTO 60
80 BEEP .2,n(VAL(a$(1)))
90 GOTO 60
```

which will allow you to play the scale of C using the top row
of number keys. Lines 10 to 50 set up an array "n" which
contains the pitch values for 8 notes. Lines 60 and 70 examine
the keyboard until a key is pressed. When this happens line 80
produces a note of fixed length of the correct pitch. This is
achieved by using the VAL function to convert the string a$ to
a number which is then used to "index" the array "n".

You should be able to extend this program to include other
keys and sharps and flats without too much trouble but if you
want to get really ambitious you will need to leave BASIC and
use machine code to speed things up.

Automatic music

The other thing that you might like to try is automatic music.
Anything very complicated is well beyond the scope of the
Spectrum and this book but you can produce some pleasing
novelties.

You might like to try completely random music:

```
10 BEEP RND,INT(20-40*RND)
20 GOTO 10
```

You should find this interesting but not for long. For a
sequence of sounds to become music you have to impose some
kind of order. A slight improvement can be brought about by
insisting that the pitch value changes by only one for each
note played.

```
10 LET p=INT(40-80*RND)
20 BEEP .1,p
30 LET p=p+SGN(.5-RND)
40 GOTO 20
```

The key line in this program is line 30 which adds or subtracts 1 to p at random. This is slightly more satisfying but even this becomes tedious after a while. Apart from this there isn't very much you can do that is simple to produce computer composed music — it's still a subject of research.

Boosting the sound

You may, by this stage, be a little tired of trying to hear the noise produced by the tiny Spectrum speaker. If so you will be pleased to hear that there is a way to hear your Spectrum music at a much higher volume without any special equipment. The sound produced by BEEP is present at both the MIC and EAR sockets at the back of the Spectrum. All you have to do is to set the tape recorder that you use to SAVE and LOAD programs to record when a piece of music or whatever is being produced by your Spectrum and it will be captured on tape. You can then rewind and play the tape at any volume you like. If you are really keen on hearing your Spectrum at volume then you could connect an amplifier and external loudspeaker to the EAR socket.

One more technical use for the Spectrum is as a sound generator. The signal coming from the EAR socket is in fact a square wave, a rather complicated expression with a frequency given by

$$f = 2^{p/12} \times fc$$

where p is the pitch value and fc is the frequency of middle C which is 261.6 cycles per second, or Hertz as it is known today. Although this is a complicated expression the Spectrum can work it out with little trouble, after all what are computers for! The following program will work out the frequency produced by any pitch value:

```
10 INPUT "pitch value =";p
20 LET f=261.6*2^(p/12)
30 PRINT "frequency = ";f;" Hz"
40 GOTO 10
```

and the following program will give the pitch value for any frequency.

```
10 INPUT "frequency in Hz = ";f
20 LET p=12*LN(f/261.6)/LN(2)
30 PRINT "Pitch value = ";p
40 GOTO 10
```

There is no particular reason why the pitch value in a BEEP command has to be a whole number. For example a quarter-tone above middle C is given by a pitch value of 0.25. You can produce any tone by using fractional pitch values.

Sound and motion

As mentioned earlier, it is not possible to produce sound and do something else at the same time. In particular, it is not possible to have sound accompany any dynamic graphics. The Spectrum is either moving something or it is making a noise — it cannot do both. The best that can be done is to move something a little bit, then make some noise, then move it again and so on. It's not entirely satisfactory but it's the best that can be done in BASIC. For example, if we want a missile to be fired accompanied by sound then the following is all we can do:

```
10 LET y=21
20 PRINT AT y,15;"^";
30 BEEP .001,50-y*2
40 LET y=y-1
50 IF y=0 THEN STOP
60 PRINT AT y+1,15;" "
70 GOTO 20
```

Lines 20 and 60 animate a small missile (an up arrow symbol) from the bottom to the top of the screen. Line 30 produces a

BEEP every time the missile is moved. As the pitch of the sound increases as the position of the missile moves up the screen, the sound seems to come from the moving shape.

You can use the same technique to produce sound and movement with a reasonable degree of success as long as the time between each movement is short. Otherwise all you hear is a series of disconnected sounds that seem to have nothing to do with the movement. One exception to this rule is the occasional beeping noise used to accompany the bouncing of a ball. The rule here is to keep the sound as short as possible. For the time that the beep lasts the ball cannot move and a ball that pauses every time it bounces looks very odd. However even a very short sound in this situation improves a game no end. If you want to see the difference try removing the BEEP command from the squash program given in Chapter Six.

It is often tempting to make a sound at every opportunity within a program. This can result in very noisy and irritating programs from the user's point of view. Only use sound when it adds something to the program. Use it to make actions such as pressing a key, bouncing a ball or hitting a target more positive or to draw the user's attention to an error message on the screen. If you use too much sound then its effect will be severely reduced.

Sound effects

There is not much that can be done with the Spectrum from BASIC to produce convincing sound effects. However there is a way of controlling the motion of the loudspeaker directly from BASIC. External equipment, such as the ZX printer, is controlled by the Spectrum using two extra commands, IN and OUT. To distinguish between different pieces of external equipment each is assigned a number — its address. The command

IN address

reads a piece of information from the external device corresponding to "address". And

OUT address,value

sends the number given by "value" to the external device corresponding to "address". The commands IN and OUT are also present in BASIC and can be used to control external devices directly as long as you know the address of the device that you are interested in.

The Spectrum's loudspeaker is an external device that has an address of 254 and this can be used in conjunction with OUT to make it click. The only extra complication is that the colour of the border surrounding the screen is also controlled as an external device — with the same address. If you want to see the effect of this confusion try the following program:

```
10 FOR i=0 TO 255
20 OUT 254,i
30 NEXT i
```

Sometimes you will see the border change colour and occasionally you will hear a click from the loudspaker. The solution to the problem lies in the fact that the value sent to the external device controls the colour or the loudspeaker according to the range that it lies in. For example, numbers between 0 and 15 affect only the colour of the border. Technically, the first three bits of the value specify the colour of the border and the fourth bit controls the loudspeaker. The only other thing that you need to know is that memory location 23624 contains the current border colour times eight. Using all this information results in the following program to make the loudspeaker click:

```
10 LET a=PEEK 23624/8
20 OUT 254,a-16
30 OUT 254,a
```

The first line of this program reads the current colour of the border (PEEK is described in more detail in Chapter 7). The first OUT in line 20 changes the state of the loudspeaker and line 30 restores it to its original state. Each time the program is run you produce a single click. If you make a loop by adding 40 GOTO 20 to the end of the program then the clicking becomes a low rasp. You can change the quality of the rasp by putting extra statements in between line 20 and 30 to create a delay. The simplest thing is to add a variable number of REMs. With some experimentation you should be able to produce a machine-gun-like noise.

Other techniques for making sound effects involve the use of clicks in conjunction with other sounds. For example a click followed by a high-pitched tone sounds like something being hit. Very low pitched sounds can be used to stand in for explosions, etc. It is surprising what you can manage using only a click and a BEEP. If you get ambitious you will still need to move to machine code but even then the method is still essentially the same. The only thing that changes is the number of clicks that you can make per second — you can make a lot more in machine code than BASIC.

Chapter Six

MOVING GRAPHICS

One of the most rewarding areas of computing is dynamic or moving graphics. It is not at all obvious how you can move from plotting a single point somewhere on the screen to making a moving display. In fact the transition is not at all difficult.

From flashing to moving

If you plot a single point and then "unplot" it again you will see a small flashing dot. Try the following program:

```
10 PLOT 100,50
20 PLOT INVERSE 1,100,50
30 GOTO 10
```

(You will have to look quite carefully to see the small dot flashing in roughly the middle of the screen.) You can get the same effect by printing a graphics block [^8] and then printing at the same place a graphics blank [8]. Try:

```
10 PRINT AT 10,10;"[^8]";
20 PRINT AT 10,10;"[8]";
30 GOTO 10
```

The flashing square produced by the use of the PRINT statement is eight times bigger than that produced by PLOT and flashes faster because the Spectrum has to do a lot less work to PRINT than the PLOT.

In either case, to alter the flashing rate you have to add delay loops. Delay LOOPS, because if you try putting only one FOR loop in — say at line 15 — the time the point is "on" will be increased but not the time that it is "off". To lengthen the "off" time you also need a FOR loop at line 25. For example, try:

```
10 INPUT ontime
20 INPUT offtime
30 PRINT AT 10,10;"[^8]";
40 FOR i=1 TO ontime
50 NEXT i
60 PRINT AT 10,10;"[8]";
70 FOR i=1 TO offtime
80 NEXT i
90 GOTO 30
```

We now know all there is to know about making things flash — but what about move? Well, the extension from flashing to moving is easy. If you plot a point and then "unplot" it and then plot the point next to it, it looks as though the "point" has "moved". If you keep on repeating the process, the point can be made to appear to move continuously. For example, let's suppose that we want to make a dot move from one side of the screen to the other in a straight line. We know how to describe a straight line from the last chapter but let's try something a little easier first. If the point moves horizontally then we simply have to increase the x co-ordinate each time we plot. Try the following:

```
10 LET y=50
20 FOR x=0 TO 255
30 PLOT x,y
40 PLOT INVERSE 1,x,y
50 NEXT x
```

This works in exactly the way we described. Line 30 plots a point; line 40 "unplots" it, then line 30 plots the point next door and so on!

When using this method you have to make sure that everything happens at just the right time to give the impression of movement at the speed that you want. In this simple example there are two times that matter, the time between plotting and "unplotting" a point and then the time between "unplotting" the old point and plotting the new point. A diagram might help to make this clear:

$$\xleftarrow{\hspace{1cm}} t_1 \xrightarrow{\hspace{1cm}} \xleftarrow{\hspace{1.5cm}} t_2 \xrightarrow{\hspace{1.5cm}}$$

```
- - - | - - - - - - - - | - - - - - - - - - - - - |
```

| point | point | next point |
| plotted | unplotted | plotted |

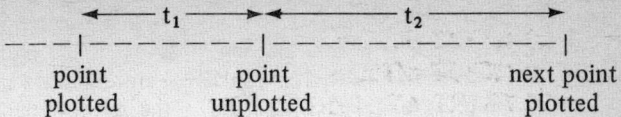

The time t_1 is the time that *any* point is displayed for and t_2 is the time that there is *no* point visible on the screen. The total time, $t_1 + t_2$ is the time it takes to move from one point to another and this governs how fast the point is seen to move. What most books on moving graphics don't tell you is what values t_1 and t_2 should have to produce a smooth display. The answer is not an easy one and in practice it is normal to change the program's values of t_1 and t_2 to produce the best possible display. It is easy to see what the values of t_1 and t_2 should be in theory. If you were watching a point moving behind a grid of holes then the time the point would be visible would correspond to t_1 and the time that the point would be hidden would correspond to t_2. If the holes of the grid were close together and regular you would still be able to see the point "moving" because the human brain tends to interpret a sequence of images as movement. What we are doing with the flashing moving point on the Spectrum's screen is to copy the principle of an object hidden behind a grid of holes and rely on the fact that the brain is fooled into seeing movement. The quality of the apparent movement on the screen can be related to how close we get to copying what is seen through the grid. If the holes are very close together then the time that the point will be seen will be large and the time that it will be hidden will be small. Put another way, t_1 will be much greater than t_2. This is the condition for producing smooth movement on the Spectrum's screen. Unfortunately this is not easy to satisfy. The Spectrum takes as long to plot as to unplot so t_2 tends to be as long as t_1. Indeed the method that we are using makes things worse. We plot a point, then unplot it, then do some calculation before we re-plot it. This actually means that t_2 is much longer than t_1. The result of this inbalance in "on" and "off" times is that the moving point tends to "twinkle" or flash as it moves. We could improve on this by plotting the point, doing the calculation and then unplotting the old point

73

and plotting the new point. The trouble is that this requires storing the old position and the new position of the plotted point and for the moment this would make programs a little more difficult to understand. To see if the improvement is worth it try:

```
10 LET y=50
20 FOR x=0 TO 255
30 PLOT INVERSE 1,x,y
40 PLOT x+1,y
50 NEXT x
```

A simpler method of making the movement smoother is to increase t_1 by putting a time-wasting element such as, 35 LET y=y, between the plot and unplot statements. This is the best method to use with the Spectrum but you might like to try some other methods.

There is something else that we can learn by thinking about viewing a moving point through a grid of holes. If the point is moving at a speed S and is invisible for a time t_2, the distance between the holes must be $S*t_2$. This suggests that, as our problem with the Spectrum is that t_2 is too big for a smooth display, we might be able to do better by increasing the distance between the displayed points! This can be done by simply plotting a point, then "unplotting" it and *instead* of plotting its next door neighbour, plotting a point further away. Try the following program:

```
10 LET y=10
20 FOR i=1 TO 10
30 FOR x=1 TO 31 STEP i
40 PRINT AT y,x;"[^8]";
50 PAUSE 5
60 PRINT AT y,x;"[8]";
70 NEXT x
80 NEXT i
```

Each time through the loop 30–70 a point moves across the screen from left to right. The first time the distance between the plotted points is 1, the next time it is 2 and so on until the distance is 10. What is interesting about this example is that, even when the point jumps by 6 or 7 points in one go, the illusion of movement remains and the smoothest movement is achieved with something around a step size of 2 or 3.

Although this larger step movement is interesting it is not always useful because many dynamic graphics programs need the point to move only one step at a time.

Bouncing balls and velocity

Now we've seen how to make a point move around the screen let's consider how to use it in more exciting and interesting ways. For a start we could plot and replot around the circumference of a circle or a square to make a point move in other than straight lines. However, let's look at a more realistic application. For dynamic games it would be useful to simulate the movement of a ball. This is best done by defining two velocities with which the ball is moving. At each movement step the plotted point (or ball) can move a number of places horizontally and a number of places vertically. Each step takes the same amount of time, so we can call the distance it moves horizontally the "horizontal velocity" and the distance it moves vertically the "vertical velocity". Thus at each movement step the horizontal velocity is added to the x co-ordinate and the vertical velocity is added to the y co-ordinate. Try the following program:

```
10 LET v=1
20 LET h=1
30 LET x=0
40 LET y=0
50 PRINT AT y,x;"[^8]"
60 PRINT AT y,x;"[8]"
70 LET x=x+h
80 LET y=y+v
90 GOTO 50
```

This program moves a ball from the top left of the screen to the bottom right and then off the screen. Because the ball shoots off the screen the program ends with an error. The obvious thing to do is to let the ball bounce around the edges of the screen — but how? The answer is surprisingly easy because we have chosen to use the horizontal and vertical velocity idea. If the ball meets a vertical wall, i.e. the right-hand edge of the screen, then it cannot carry on moving in the same horizontal direction. In fact nothing but a complete reversal of horizontal velocity will stop it going through the wall! The vertical velocity is not affected by meeting a vertical wall — why should it be?! So the rule is: when the ball meets a vertical wall reverse the horizontal velocity. Similarly when the ball meets a horizontal wall reverse the vertical velocity. Using these two rules we have:

```
10 LET v=1
20 LET h=1
30 LET x=0
40 LET y=0
50 PRINT AT y,x;"[^8]"
60 PRINT AT y,x;"[8]"
70 LET x=x+h
80 LET y=y+v
90 IF x=0 OR x=31 THEN LET h=-h
100 IF y=0 OR y=21 THEN LET v=-v
110 GOTO 50
```

This is a remarkably simply program for the effect it achieves. Lines 90 and 100 test for the presence of a horizontal or vertical wall. If one is found then the appropriate velocity is reversed. (If you haven't already worked it out, reversing a velocity is the same thing as putting a minus sign in front of it.) Because of their different ways of numbering the screen positions, if you're using PRINT AT statements positive velocities take you from the *top* to the *bottom* of the screen, but if you're using PLOT statements they go from *bottom* to *top*.

Although this program is impressive it can still be improved! The first thing is that the moving ball flashes a little

76

more than it needs to. The time between displaying it on the screen and then removing it can be increased by moving line 50 to 85 (remembering to change line 110 to GOTO 60!) If you try this you should find the movement a lot smoother. The next improvement is to include a BEEP every time the ball is bounced. To do this change lines 90 and 100 to read:

```
90 IF x=0 OR x=31 THEN LET h=h-1:BEEP .01,10
100 IF y=0 OR y=21 THEN LET v=v-1:BEEP .01,10
```

This simple change is well worth making as it seems to make the bouncing more positive. However it also alerts us to another problem. The ball appears to pause each time it bounces. If you would like to change the duration of the BEEP from .01 to .1 then you will see this very clearly. The reason is simply that there is more computing to do if the ball bounces than if it doesn't. To even things up you have to include a delay in the normal movement of the ball, that is as long as the time it takes for the ball to bounce. In other words, you must make each movement step take the same amount of time, bounce or no bounce. The final program is:

```
10 LET v=1
20 LET h=1
30 LET x=0
40 LET y=0
60 PRINT AT y,x;"[8]"
70 LET x=x+h
80 LET y=y+v
85 PRINT AT y,x;"[^8]"
90 IF x=0 OR x=31 THEN LET h=-h:
   BEEP .01,10:GOTO 60
100 IF y=0 OR y=21 THEN LET v=-v:
   BEEP .01,10:GOTO 60
105 PAUSE 3
110 GOTO 60
```

(Notice that the lines in this program are not numbered in even jumps of 10 to enable it to be compared to the previous program.) The PAUSE 3 in line 105 is only carried out if the ball doesn't bounce. The length of the PAUSE was adjusted by trial and error to make the ball move as smoothly as possible. Notice however that this does make the whole program run very much slower — perfection has its price!

Now that you know how to make a ball move and bounce it might seem sensible to try to write a bat-and-ball-type game. After all, striking the ball with a bat follows the rules for reversing velocity as does the ball striking a wall. This is indeed what we shall do next!

Squash

As an example of a "bouncing ball" program consider the squash program given below.

```
10 LET ball=0
20 GOSUB 800
30 INK 0:PAPER 6:CLS
40 LET a=10:LET b=10
50 LET v=1:LET w=1
60 LET x=10:LET y=21
70 LET ball=ball+1
80 GOSUB 500
90 PRINT ball
100 GOSUB 200
110 GOSUB 700
120 GOSUB 300
130 IF b<>21 THEN GOTO 100
140 BEEP .5,-10
150 GOTO 30

200 LET a$=INKEY$
210 IF a$="5" AND x>0 THEN LET x=x-1
220 IF a$="8" AND x<27 THEN LET x=x+1
230 RETURN

300 PRINT AT b,a;"[8]";
```

78

```
310 LET a=a+v
320 LET b=b+w
330 IF a=31 OR a=0 THEN LET v=-v:BEEP .01,10
340 IF b=1 THEN LET w=-w:BEEP .01,10
350 IF b+1=y THEN GOSUB 400
360 PRINT AT b,a;"[a]";
370 RETURN

400 LET r=a-x
410 IF r<1 OR r>3 THEN RETURN
420 LET w=-w
430 BEEP .01,0
440 RETURN

500 FOR i=0 TO 31
510 PRINT AT 0,i;"[^8]";
520 NEXT i
530 RETURN

700 PRINT AT y,x;"[8][^8][^8][^8][8]";
710 RETURN

800 POKE USR "a"+0,BIN 00111100
810 POKE USR "a"+1,BIN 01111110
820 POKE USR "a"+2,BIN 11111111
830 POKE USR "a"+3,BIN 11111111
840 POKE USR "a"+4,BIN 11111111
850 POKE USR "a"+5,BIN 11111111
860 POKE USR "a"+6,BIN 01111110
870 POKE USR "a"+7,BIN 00111100
880 RETURN
```

This is a simple application of the moving graphics methods that have been introduced. The program starts by defining a ball shape in subroutine 800 and then prints the wall of the court using subroutine 500. Subroutine 300 plots the ball at

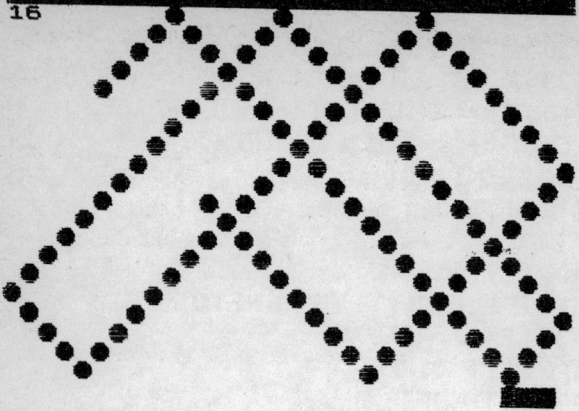

location a,b and keeps track of the ball's horizontal velocity v and vertical velocity w. If the ball hits a "wall", i.e. tries to go off the screen, then the correct velocity is reversed to make it bounce. Subroutine 700 prints the bat at location x,y. Notice that erasing the old bat is unnecessary because of the two blanks included at each end of the bat. The only two new features are the way that the bat is moved and the way the ball is made to bounce off the bat. To move the bat all that is necessary is to change the bat's horizontal co-ordinate according to which key is pressed. If the left-arrow key is pressed then one is subtracted from x, moving the bat one place to the left. If the right-arrow key is pressed then one is added to x, moving the bat one place to the right. All this is done by subroutine 200. Before each update of the bat's position a check is made to make sure that it is still on the screen. The ball bouncing off the bat is carried out by sub-routine 400. If the ball is at the same vertical position as the bat then line 350 calls subroutine 400 to check if it has the correct horizontal position to be bounced, i.e. have its vertical velocity reversed. If the ball goes off the screen at the bottom (detected by line 130) then control passes to line 100 and a new game is started. Notice that the game is played by lines 100 to 130 being repeated over and over again. Line 100 calls the move bat routine, line 110 actually moves the bat and line 120 calls the routines that look after the ball and its bouncing.

Free flight and gravity

The previous section discussed moving a ball around inside a frame and how it could be made to bounce. There is another way in which a ball can move — it can be thrown through the air. Let's try to find a way of making a ball move under the influence of gravity.

In outer space, where there is no gravity, a ball set moving in a particular direction with a particular velocity will carry on moving in the same direction and at the same velocity forever! (Unless it hits some other object and then it would bounce off in the opposite direction at the same velocity, like the ball in the previous section.) In this sense, the way that we know how to move a ball at the moment corresponds to gravity-free movement. Let's write a program that simulates a ball thrown without any gravity.

```
10 LET v=0
20 LET h=1
30 LET x=0
40 LET y=0
50 PRINT AT y,x;"[^8]"
60 PRINT AT y,x;"[8]"
70 LET x=x+h
90 LET y=y+v
100 GOTO 50
```

If you look at lines 10 and 20 you should be able to see that the ball is thrown horizontally forward from the top of the screen. It's rather like pushing a ball off the top of a cliff — only in this case where there is no gravity, instead of falling it moves in a straight line, totally unaffected by anything.

If we introduce gravity the difference is that the vertical velocity changes. For example, if you just release a ball it falls and its vertical velocity increases as it falls faster and faster. In other words as the ball moves one unit horizontally its vertical velocity increases by a fixed amount. The value of the fixed amount depends upon how strong gravity is but for our purpose we can adjust it so that it gives a reasonable result. To see the falling ball add line 80:

80 LET v=v+.1

to the "free fall' program. When run, the new program mimics a ball falling in a parabolic curve. The program gives an error as soon as the ball "falls" off the bottom of the screen. If you want to improve the program try subtracting a small amount from the horizontal velocity to allow for wind resistance.

We can combine what we already know about bouncing balls with what we have just discovered about gravity. If we define a horizontal wall, at say y=15, then as the ball reaches it we can apply our previous "bounce" rule and reverse the vertical velocity. The resulting program is:

```
10 LET v=0
20 LET h=1
30 LET x=0
40 LET y=0
50 PRINT AT y,x;"[^8]"
60 PRINT AT y,x;"[8]"
70 LET x=x+h
80 LET v=v+.6
90 LET y=y+v
100 IF y>15 THEN LET v=-v
110 GOTO 50
```

If you remove line 60 then the output looks something like; that shown at the top of page 83.

By now you should have a good idea how to make a ball do anything that you want it to. Using the horizontal and vertical velocity idea everything is quite simple. If you want to speed up the ball then add something to the appropriate velocity or subtract to slow it down.

Lunar lander

If we add a few extras to the falling ball program described in the last section we can produce a reasonable lunar landing game. A rocket landing on the Moon behaves exactly like a falling ball except that it can fire its motors and reduce its vertical velocity.

```
10 LET f=1200
20 GOSUB 300
30 LET b=0:LET v=0
40 LET h=RND
50 LET x=0
60 LET y=1
70 PRINT AT y,x;"[a]";
80 GOSUB 170
90 PAUSE 3:PRINT AT y,x;"[8]";
100 LET x=x+h
110 IF x>30 THEN GOSUB 250
120 LET y=y+v
130 IF y<19 THEN GOTO 70
140 IF v>.5 THEN PRINT AT 10,10;"**Crash**"
150 IF v<=.5 THEN PRINT AT 10,3;
    "**Spectrum has landed**"
160 STOP
```

83

```
170 LET b$=INKEY$
180 IF b$="" THEN GOTO 200
190 LET b=VAL b$ *10
200 LET f=f-b
210 IF f<0 THEN LET b=0
220 LET v=v-b/1000+.05
230 PRINT AT 0,0;"H= ";INT(11.6*(19-y));
   " S=";INT(200*v);" F=";f;" BR=";b;"   "
240 RETURN

250 LET x=0
260 CLS
270 GOTO 380

300 POKE USR "a"+0,BIN 00011000
310 POKE USR "a"+1,BIN 00111100
320 POKE USR "a"+2,BIN 01111110
330 POKE USR "a"+3,BIN 11111111
340 POKE USR "a"+4,BIN 00011000
350 POKE USR "a"+5,BIN 00111100
360 POKE USR "a"+6,BIN 00111100
370 POKE USR "a"+7,BIN 00000000
380 FOR i=0 TO 31
390 PRINT AT 21,i;"[3]";
400 NEXT i
410 RETURN
```

The amount of fuel that you start with is set in line 10. If you
want to make the game easier increase the amount of fuel
from 1200 to something larger. The rocket starts with a
random horizontal velocity, set in line 40, and falls under
gravity until it hits the ground. As it falls you can burn fuel to
reduce its rate of descent. Pressing any key between 0 and 9
sets the rate at which fuel is burned — the burn rate BR. the
burn rate is ten times the value of the key pressed. Which key
is pressed is checked at line 170 using the INKEY$ statement.
Keep pressing the key that you want because it will only affect

the program once every time the rocket moves. The fuel
burned is subtracted from the fuel remaining and if you use it
all up you free fall to the surface. The object of the game is
to land with a vertical velocity of less than 100 metres per
second. If you move too far to the right the screen is cleared
and you start from the far left again. Happy landings!

Throwing in a given direction

So far we have found how a ball moves under gravity if thrown
horizontally from a cliff but many games need a ball to be
thrown upward. This can be achieved by reversing the y co-
ordinates in a PRINT AT or simply using a PLOT statement
instead. Remember that PLOT 0,0 is the *bottom* left but
PRINT AT 0,0 is the *top* left. Try the following:

```
10 LET x=0
20 LET y=0
30 LET h=2
40 LET v=4
50 PLOT x,y:PLOT x+1,y
60 PLOT INVERSE 1,x,y:
   PLOT INVERSE 1,x+1,y
70 LET x=x+h
```

```
80 LET v=v-.1
90 LET y=y+v
100 IF y<1 THEN STOP
110 GOTO 50
```

The initial velocity is h=2 and v=4. At each step the vertical velocity is reduced by .1. So the ball first starts moving up quite fast then slows down until it is only moving forward. Then the vertical direction is reversed and the ball starts falling down back to the bottom of the screen. Notice also that two points are plotted to make it easier to see. The resulting shape is the well-known parabola of a thrown object.

Normally we want to throw a ball at a given angle and with a given force. If we throw the ball with a given force this governs its overall velocity. That is, the harder you throw a ball the faster it moves at first. The angle at which you throw it alters the distribution of this overall velocity between the vertical and horizontal parts. For example, if you throw the ball straight up at 90 degrees then the ball moves vertically but not horizontally. As you decrease the angle the ball moves more horizontally and less vertically. If you analyse the situation mathematically you will find that, if you throw the ball with a force that produces a total velocity v at an angle t, then the horizontal velocity is given by $v*COS(t)$ and the vertical velocity is given by $v*SIN(t)$. Using these two starting values for horizontal and vertical velocity we can use the same sort of program to make the ball move under gravity. The only thing that we have to remember is that the Spectrum measures angles in radians. To convert degrees to radians use angle in radians = angle in degrees$*PI/180$.

Cannon-ball

Now that we know how to throw something at a given angle and with a given force, we can try to write a shooting game. You have a cannon set at the far left-hand side of the screen and a target randomly placed to the right. You have to specify two numbers -- the angle 0—90 degrees and the force of the charge -- and try to hit the target. The force of the charge is unlimited but values around 10 work well. An additional problem is that if you shoot at such an angle that the cannon-ball leaves the screen *anywhere* it is counted as a miss. This means that you have to fire the cannon at a low angle to make sure that you do not shoot off the top of the screen! This restriction also stops you from shooting down any of your own aircraft! You'll find low angle shots more difficult so the limitation actually improves the game.

```
10 LET b=30
20 GOSUB 300
30 INPUT "Force=";f
40 LET f=f/2
50 INPUT "Angle=";t
60 LET h=f*COS(t*PI/180)
70 LET v=f*SIN(t*PI/180)
80 LET x=0
90 LET y=b
100 PLOT x,y:PLOT x,y+1
110 LET v=v-.1
120 PLOT INVERSE 1,x,y:PLOT INVERSE 1,x,y+1
130 LET x=x+h
140 LET y=y+v
150 IF y<=b THEN GOTO 200
160 IF x>255 OR y>150 THEN GOTO 200
170 GOTO 100

200 IF x>=p AND x<=p+10 THEN GOTO 250
```

```
210 LET m=m+1
220 GOTO 260

250 BEEP .2,.10:LET s=s+1
260 PRINT AT 1,0;"hit=";s;" miss=";m;"        "
270 GOTO 30

300 LET p=RND*100+100
310 PLOT p,b
320 DRAW 10,0
330 LET m=0
340 LET s=0
350 RETURN
```

`hits=1  miss=3`

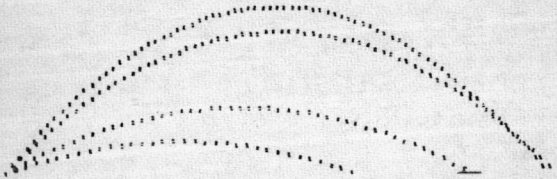

Subroutine 300 plots the target at a random position 10 points wide and initialises m and s, the miss and score counters. Lines 30 to 50 input f the force and t the angle. The force is scaled in line 40 to give a reasonable range of velocities. The middle section is simply the thrown ball program given earlier in this section but with extra statements to check if the ball has hit the target.

It is possible to write much more complicated programs along these lines, to allow for such things as air resistance and wind direction – so experiment!

Conclusion

You should now be in a position to expand and improve programs such as lunar lander and squash and to use them as the basis of your own games. Add sound, scoring and extra difficulties for the player. You could, for example, try writing a two person version of squash with two bats.

Chapter Seven

PEEK AND POKE

Two of the most mysterious instructions in the whole of
BASIC are PEEK and POKE. The question: "What can I use
PEEK and POKE for?" is frequently asked. The answer
depends very much on which computer you are using. This
chapter gives a brief explanation of what PEEK and POKE
do and examples of how they can be used on the Spectrum.
Do not expect what you learn here about how to use PEEK
and POKE to apply to other computers — it almost invariably
will not!

What PEEK and POKE do

Of the two instructions, PEEK is the easier to understand and
the safer to use. You cannot crash the machine with an in-
correct use of PEEK but you most certainly can with POKE.
Although we have referred to PEEK as an instruction it is
more properly called a "function" because it returns a result.
(Functions are things like SIN(x) which can be worked out to
some number — the result.) PEEK is a special sort of function
in that it doesn't "work" anything out it simply "returns"
the contents of a particular memory location and converts it
to decimal. For example:

10 LET a=PEEK 7688

will set a to the contents of memory location 7688. There are
many things that you will need to know about computers in
general, and the Spectrum in particular, before this example
will make very much sense to you. Firstly, you have to know
that computers save and retrieve information from numbered
memory locations. Each location has a unique number, known
as its "address". Secondly, you need to know that the amount
of information that can be stored at each location is limited.
In the case of the Spectrum each memory location can only

store one character. As you probably already know a computer can only store zeros or ones in its memory so how does it manage to store an actual character in a memory location? The answer is that a group of bits (zeros or ones) can be read as a number. For example 0101 is five. It's not important at the moment that you know how to convert a group of bits, it's sufficient to know that it can be done. (If you want to find out how, see *Beginners Guide to Microprocessors and Computing* – BP66, by E. F. Scott.) A group of 8 bits – a byte, can represent numbers from 0 (00000000) to 255 (11111111), so any Spectrum memory location can be thought of as holding a number in this range. At this point you should realize how a character is stored as a group of 8 bits!

If you look at the back of the Spectrum manual you will find a list of the Spectrum character set. The first column is labelled "code" and contains numbers starting at 0 and going up to 255. This means that we can either treat the contents of a memory location as a number, 76 say, or as the character CHR$(76) which gives L. The most important thing to understand though is that any Spectrum memory location may contain a number between 0 and 255. If you add PRINT a to the earlier example you will see that this is true, i.e. a lies between 0 and 255. If you look at the contents of any other memory location you will see many different numbers but none of them smaller than 0 or greater than 255.

The only other thing that you need to know about using PEEK is the range of addresses that you can use. The Spectrum numbers its memory locations starting at 0 and going up to a maximum of 65535. Not all of these memory locations correspond to anything in the Spectrum; as we shall see later, many of them are unused. One last fact it is important to know, is that there are two types of memory – RAM and ROM. RAM – Random Access Memory, can be used to store and recall information. ROM – Read Only Memory, can only be used to recall information. A 16K Spectrum has around 16000 memory locations that correspond to RAM but has an equal number of memory locations that correspond to ROM. This vast quantity of inbuilt information in every Spectrum is used for many different things but one of the main uses is to define the rules of the BASIC language. The ROM portion of memory starts at 0 and goes up to 16383. The RAM portion starts at 16384 and goes up to 32767 if you have 16K of RAM or 65535 if you have 48K. In a full 48K machine all the memory locations are assigned to either ROM or RAM.

The POKE instruction is easy if you have followed the explanation of how PEEK works. POKE allows you to store a byte in any RAM memory location. Doing this may destroy your program if it happens to be stored in a location that you already use – so take care! The form of POKE is.

POKE address,byte

For example, if you type in (no line numbers because you want the computer to carry out the command at once and you don't want a program in memory that might get in the way!).

POKE 17300,33
PRINT PEEK 17300

You should (if your Spectrum is working) see 33 printed out on the screen. What you have done is to store a pattern of bits representing 33 in the memory location whose address is 17300 and then printed out its contents. Try the same thing with different data bytes to convince yourself that it works. If you try a POKE at addresses that correspond to ROM you wont't get very far – for obvious reasons!

Using PEEK to draw big letters

One interesting and useful part of the ROM area of memory is the character generator. If you use PRINT "A" somehow or other the Spectrum has to construct a pattern of ink and paper dots on the screen corresponding to the shape of the letter A. To do this it looks the pattern up in a table stored in the ROM region of memory. This table is called the character generator and contains a pattern of dots for the shape of every character that the Spectrum can print. We have already seen how a pattern of dots can be represented as a pattern of noughts and ones when we looked at user-defined graphics in Chapter Two.

If we use eight memory locations per character then we can store eight rows of eight dots used to draw a character. For example the letter A would be:

pattern of bits	decimal number
0 0 0 0 0 0 0 0	0
0 0 1 1 1 1 0 0	60
0 1 0 0 0 0 1 0	66
0 1 0 0 0 0 1 0	66
0 1 1 1 1 1 1 0	126
0 1 0 0 0 0 1 0	66
0 1 0 0 0 0 1 0	66
0 0 0 0 0 0 0 0	00

If you find the A difficult to see then try colouring in all the ones. The letter is surrounded by zeros to make sure that there is some space around each letter when it's printed. The column of decimal numbers corresponds to what would be printed out by PEEKing the memory locations where the shape of A is stored.

The problem of where the character generator is in ROM is easily solved by reference to Chapter 25 of the Spectrum manual. This reveals that the address of the start of the table is stored in memory locations 23606 and 23607. In fact it is the correct address less 256 for a reason that need not worry us. So to find the start of the character generator all we have to do is PEEK the contents of the two memory locations. A number bigger than 255 can be stored in two memory locations but it has to be split up into two parts each less than 255. (We will look at how this is achieved later.) To reconstruct the number it is necessary to use the statement

PEEK a +256*PEEK(a+1)

where a is the address of the first (i.e. lower) of the two memory locations. In the Spectrum manual it also states that the character table begins with the space character and continues up to the copyright symbol i.e. CHR$(127). Knowing that each character's definition takes eight memory locations you should be able to see that the definition of character CHR$(i) is at memory location

start +8*(i−32)

where "start" is the start of the character table.

Knowing where the character generator table is stored in ROM means that we can write a program to use the dot patterns to print or plot points to make larger characters. To do this we have to solve a number of problems. We can use PEEK to find the number stored in any location but we need to know the pattern of ones and zeros. In other words, we have to find a way to reduce a number to its sequence of zeros and ones. This is not difficult to do if you understand binary numbers and arithmetic. To avoid getting involved in too much theory we will simply use the following program, which simply gives a line of eight noughts, without detailed explanation.

```
10 LET start=256+PEEK 23606+256*PEEK 23607
20 LET a=start+8*(65-32)
30 LET r=PEEK a
40 FOR i=7 TO 0 STEP -1
50 LET b=r-2*INT(r/2)
60 LET r=INT(r/2)
70 PRINT AT 20,i;b
80 NEXT i
```

You should be able to see that a contains the address of the start of the 8 bytes that define the letter A. Line 30 PEEKs the dot pattern for the first row of the letter A into the variable called r. Each time through the FOR loop we extract one bit from r and print it. The first time through we extract the left-most bit, then the next left-most and so on until we have printed all 8 bits. The FOR loop goes from 7 to 0 because we want to print the result from left to right and the index i is used in the PRINT AT 20,i. You can get the whole pattern for r by repeating the program eight times, once for each row of the letter A.

```
10 LET start=256+PEEK 23606+256*PEEK 23607
20 LET a=start+8*(65-32)
```

```
30 FOR j=0 TO 7
40 LET r=PEEK(a+j)
50 FOR i=7 TO 0 STEP -1
60 LET b=r-2*INT(r/2)
70 LET r=INT(r/2)
80 PRINT AT 21,i;b
90 NEXT i
100 PRINT
110 NEXT j
```

If you answer "y" to "Scroll?", you should be able to see the
dot pattern of the letter A when you run this program. Now
we are nearly home and dry! All we have to do is to add some
statements to print a blank when b is 0 and a black square
when b is one and we have a large letter A on the screen.
Add some code to pick out the appropriate part of the table
for any particular string of letters and we can have large
messages moving up the screen. Try the following:

```
10 INPUT a$
20 LET start=256+PEEK 23606+256*PEEK 23607
30 FOR i=1 TO LEN a$
40 LET a=start+8*((CODE a$(i))-32)
50 FOR j=0 TO 7
60 LET r=PEEK(a+j)
70 FOR k=7 TO 0 STEP -1
80 PRINT AT 21,k;CHR$(128+15*(r-2*INT(r/2)))
90 LET r=INT(r/2)
100 NEXT k
110 PRINT
120 NEXT j
130 NEXT i
```

If you type in any message it will be displayed as a sequence of
moving big letters up the left-hand side of the screen.

Spectrum

Line 40 picks out the position in the table of each letter. The table starts at the address stored in "start" and the character CHR$(32) i.e. blank is the first. The function CODE is the opposite of CHR$. It takes a letter and returns its position in the character set. Each letter takes eight memory locations, so you have to multiply the character code by eight to get to the right place in the table. Line 80 uses the same method introduced in the earlier program to decide if we have a zero or a one, but this time instead of printing zero or one, it prints CHR$(128+15*0) i.e. the blank graphics character [8], or CHR$(128+15*1) i.e. the full graphics character [^8]. If you want to repeat the message forever add

130 GOTO 20
140 GOTO 20

You could use this last program to add large letter outputs to any program.

Manipulating memory locations

As already discussed, a single memory location can hold a number between 0 and 255 and as we have already seen, there is often a need to store numbers larger than this in a computer. For example, the address of a Spectrum memory location can lie between 0 and 65534. So, to store a single address we have to use *two* memory locations. The way that this works is based on the principles of binary numbers, but from the point of view of a BASIC programmer this is an unnecessary complication and it is best understood, and easier to remember, in terms of the decimal numbers that are used in programming statements. The largest number that a single memory location or byte can hold is 255. So if you use a single memory location to count, you can start at zero and count quite happily until you reach 255. If you try to add one to 255 you cannot store the answer 256 in a single memory location but you could store one in another memory location to indicate that you have reached 256 once. You could then carry on counting in the first memory location as if nothing had happened (starting again at zero) until you reach 255 again. In fact, what you are doing is to use the second memory location as a count of the number of times that you have reached 256. The first memory location counts single things and is known as the "least significant byte" and the second memory location counts 256s and is known as the "most significant byte".

first memory location units	second memory location 256s
least significant	most significant

It should now be obvious how to "reconstruct" an address from two memory locations. As the first counts units, we can just PEEK its value but the second counts 256s so its value must be multiplied by 256 before it is added to the first value. Translating this into BASIC gives

PEEK m +256*PEEK(m+1)

as the way of finding out what is stored in two memory locations, the address of the first being stored in m. Going the other way is just as easy. If you want to split a number up so that it can be stored in two memory locations, first divide it by 256 to find out how many 256s it contains and store the result in the most significant byte and then store the remainder in the least significant byte. That is

POKE m+1,INT(v/256)
POKE m,v−256*INT(v/256)

will store the number v in the two memory locations m and m+1. We have already used the method of PEEKing two memory locations. In the next section we will see that memory locations sometimes have to be POKEed!

Some useful memory locations

If you look at Chapter 25 of the Spectrum manual you will see a list of memory locations and what they are used for. Many of these locations serve purposes that are of no interest to the

BASIC programmer. However some of them can be very useful indeed. A selection of the most useful is discussed below.

Auto Repeat Delay — the time a key has to be held down before it auto repeats can be set by POKEing location 23561 with the delay in 50ths of a second.

Key Repeat Rate — the rate at which the keys auto repeat can be altered by POKEing the new rate in 50ths of a second into 23562.

Both of these memory locations are useful if you want to increase the responsiveness of the keyboard while playing games.

Keypress Beep — the length of the keypress click can be set by POKEing 23609. If you increase this sufficiently the click that normally accompanies every keypress becomes a beep.

Start of User-defined graphics — memory locations 23675 and 23676 hold the address of the start of the area of RAM used to store the definitions of the user-defined characters.

X and Y co-ordinates of the last plotted point — can be found in 23677 and 23678 respectively. These can be PEEKed by a program to find out where the last plotted point was or POKEed to alter where DRAW starts from.

Scroll suppression — the memory location 23692 counts how many times the screen has automatically moved up by one line i.e. scrolled. More accurately it counts the number of scrolls before the "Scroll?" message appears on the screen. If this message is a nuisance, as it is in the big letter program given earlier, it can be suppressed by POKEing a large value (255 say) into this location every now and again. For example, to stop the "Scroll?" message appearing in the big letter program add

```
35 POKE 23692,255
```

Conclusion

This chapter has tried to give some idea of the way that PEEK and POKE work. The example of using PEEK to display large letters is typical of the sorts of things that PEEK and POKE are used for. Notice that, apart from knowing how PEEK works, the example requires knowledge about the machine, i.e. the fact that a character generator exists, where it is and what its format is. These extra pieces of information sometimes become confused with knowing how PEEK and POKE work. If you move to a new machine then the way PEEK and POKE work will remain the same but the big letter program will not work. It might be possible to change it so that it works if you know where the character generator is etc. By now you should be able to understand that there is no answer to the question "what are PEEK and POKE used for" unless you say which machine you're talking about.

Chapter Eight

A SENSE OF TIME

Every computer has a way of keeping time, built into it. Some make it easy for a programmer to get at it, others make it nearly impossible. The Spectrum is somewhere in between these two extremes in that it provides a timing command — PAUSE which allows you access to its clock — but for any really useful timing you have to use a PEEK and the occasional POKE. Before going on to examine methods of using time let's see what makes the Spectrum tick.

An internal clock

The Spectrum's microprocessor, the Z80 is responsible for maintaining the screen display. A standard television set displays a picture every 1/50th of a second (1/60th of a second in the USA) so the Spectrum has to stop whatever it is doing every 1/50th of a second and display the TV screen.

The Spectrum's internal "clock" is actually a very handy facility that we can make good use of. The PAUSE command is one way of doing so. For example try the following program:

```
10 PRINT"tick"
20 PAUSE 50
30 PRINT"tock"
40 PAUSE 50
60 GOTO 10
```

This will print "tick tock" on the screen at about one-second intervals. The only problem with this program is that although each PAUSE causes a pause for 1 second (i.e. 50 frames) the time between each tick and tock is longer because the computer takes time to PRINT and GOTO.

101

Delay loops

Many computers do not have a PAUSE command and so it is useful to know another way to create a fixed delay — the delay loop. A delay loop is simply a FOR loop that does nothing but waste a fixed and known amount of time. For example:

```
10 LET t=200
20 PRINT "tick"
30 FOR i=1 TO t
40 NEXT i
50 PRINT "tock"
60 FOR i=1 TO t
70 NEXT i
80 GOTO 10
```

Two delay loops are included in this program. Each gives a delay of slightly less than one second and this makes the time between each "tick" and "tock" roughly one second. If you want to check the accuracy and regulate the clock, the best way is to time a large number of "tick-tocks" and work out how long each takes. If it's less than a second then increase t and vice versa. Notice that the time delay depends on the type of statement used as a delay loop. If you change FOR i=1 TO t to FOR i=1 TO 200, the time that the loop takes will change very slightly.

The frame counter

As the Spectrum can PAUSE and display a given number of TV frames you may have guessed that somewhere inside it is a memory location that counts the number of frames that have been displayed. In fact there are three memory locations that keep track of the number of frames and these together are known as the FRAME COUNTER. The frame counter is at addresses 23674, 23673 and 23672. The memory location at address 23672 counts the number of frames since the machine was switched on. As the largest number that a

102

single memory location can hold is 255 the number of frames that location 23672 can count is limited. To overcome this problem location 23673 counts the number of times the lower location reaches 255. In other words, the lower location counts frames and the higher location counts every 256 frames, i.e. the lower counter goes from 0—255 for every one count of the upper counter. This is very like a traditional clock dial, with the lower counter going "round" every 256 and then moving the upper counter on one. In the same way every time address 23673 reaches 255 the next memory location i.e. 23674 has one added to it. To summarise the first location counts every 50th of a second, the second every 256*50th of a second and the last every 256*256*50th of a second.

To see the counters working try:

```
10 PRINT PEEK(23672)+256*PEEK(23673)+
   65536*PEEK(23674)
20 GOTO 10
```

(Note that 256*256 is 65536.) The difference between successive values is the number of frames that the Spectrum displays in between each print. To see the same number in terms of seconds all we have to do is divide by 50. If we also want to zero the clock at the start of the program we have to POKE zero into the three locations. For example:

```
10 LET p=23672
20 POKE p+2,0
30 POKE p+1,0
40 POKE p,0
50 PRINT PEEK(p)+256*PEEK(p+1)+
   65536*PEEK(p+2)
```

After setting to zero, to continue counting add line 60.

```
60 GOTO 50
```

Notice that it's a good idea to POKE the fastest changing counter last — just as when you set a clock you deal with the hours first, then the minutes and finally the seconds.

Digital clock

There are many ways to turn the Spectrum into a digital clock. One of the easiest is to use the program in the previous section to provide the number of seconds since the machine was switched on. All you have to do is add the current time in seconds, convert the answer to hours, minutes and seconds and display the result. A more interesting method is based on the "tick-tock" program. Instead of using the frame counter to keep track of the time why not use it to signal that one second has passed. Try the following program:

```
10 LET p=23673
20 POKE p,0
30 IF PEEK p<>50 THEN GOTO 30
40 POKE p,50
50 PRINT "tick"
60 GOTO 30
```

Before you decide that there has been a misprint, let me point out that *this program does not work!* The reason why it doesn't work is what interests us. It is difficult to see why the program fails because the idea behind it seems foolproof. At line 20 the lower frame counter is set to 0. At line 30 the value of the lower frame counter is checked to see if it's reached fifty. If it's not then the program checks again. If it is fifty then we know that fifty frames have been displayed and one second has passed. The counter is immediately reset and begins to count out the next second while we print "tick" on the screen. Why doesn't this work? There is certainly plenty of time to get to the IF statement before the count reaches 0 — not even the Spectrum needs a whole second to carry out two lines of BASIC. The trouble lies in the IF statement itself. The IF statement takes longer than 1/50 second to complete! This means that when the frame counter changes to 50 the program might only just have finished working out the result of the last PEEK! If you run the program often you might just see one "tick" printed on the screen because by chance the IF statement happened to read the frame counter just as it reached 50.

If you want to use the frame counter as an internal timer then you have to choose a time interval that is long compared to the length of time that an IF statement takes to execute. The upper frame counter changes only once every 256 frames or every 5.12 seconds. If you are prepared to have a clock tick only every 5.12 seconds then you can use the upper frame counter in the sort of program that fails using the lower frame counter. Try the following:

```
10 LET s=0
20 LET h=20
30 LET m=39
40 LET p=23673
50 POKE p,0
60 LET a=PEEK p
70 LET b=a
80 LET a=PEEK p
90 IF a=b THEN GOTO 80
100 LET s=s+5.12
110 IF s<60 THEN GOTO 190
120 LET s=s-60
130 LET m=m+1
140 IF m<60 THEN GOTO 190
150 LET m=0
160 LET h=h+1
170 IF h<24 THEN GOTO 190
180 LET h=0
190 CLS
200 PRINT AT 0,0;h;AT 0,3;m;AT 0,6;INT s
210 GOTO 70
```

The program works by reading the upper frame counter at line 60 and then reading it again at line 80 and waiting until the difference is one. When this happens 5.12 seconds have passed and the second counter can be updated at line 100 and the time re-displayed by lines 110–200. This program starts the clock at 20:39 hours. To set a different time alter the values for seconds, hours and minutes in lines 10 to 30.

There is obviously a lot that can be done to this program to improve it — for example, you might like to add the large letter displays given in chapter Seven or an alarm clock facility. However if you decide to add a clicking noise using BEEP to imitate a tick-tock then notice that the frame counters stop counting during BEEP!

A chess clock

A simple application of the frame counter is a chess clock:

```
10 LET tw=0
20 LET tb=0
30 LET g=0
40 LET p=23672
50 PRINT "Press any key to start game"
60 IF INKEY$="" THEN GOTO 60
70 CLS
80 POKE p+2,0:POKE p+1,0:POKE p,0
90 LET t=(PEEK(p)+256*PEEK(p+1)+
     65536*PEEK(p+2))/50
100 IF g=1 THEN PRINT AT 5,15;"BLACK ";
     INT((t+tb)/60);".";INT((t+tb)-
     INT((t+tb)/60)*60);"   "
110 IF g=0 THEN PRINT AT 5,0;"WHITE ";
     INT((t+tw)/60);".";INT((t+tw)-
     INT((t+tw)/60)*60);"   "
120 IF INKEY$="" THEN GOTO 90
130 BEEP .1,0
140 IF g=0 THEN LET tw=tw+t
150 IF g=1 THEN LET tb=tb+t
160 LET g=NOT g
170 GOTO 80
```

There is nothing really new in this program and you should be able to spot some techniques from earlier chapters. The total

106

move time is kept in tw for white and tb for black. The variable g is 1 if black is playing and 0 if white is. Pressing any key switches players (line 120). The time t since the last switch is added to the correct total play time in lines 100 and 110 for black and white respectively and then the timer is reset at line 80. The only limitation on this chess clock is that any move must take less than 4 days otherwise the frame counter reaches its maximum count and starts counting again!

Reaction time game.

Using the lower frame counter it is possible to time events to 1/50 of a second. This makes it just feasible to write a reaction time program. It is important to realise that, because of the slowness of Spectrum BASIC, the accuracy of the reaction times measured is worse than 1/50th of a second. This is not good enough for any serious purpose but it is fun.

```
10 PRINT "ready"
20 FOR i=0 TO RND*100+50
30 NEXT i
40 LET p=23672
50 POKE p+1,0
60 POKE p,0
70 PRINT "go"
80 IF INKEY$="" THEN GOTO 80
90 LET t=PEEK(p)+PEEK(p+1)*256
100 PRINT "Reaction time=";t/50;"sec"
110 GOTO 10
```

After a random delay the word "go" is printed. Pressing any key causes the time to be read and printed out. The program can be made more interesting and accurate by taking the average of 10 reaction time measurements. After you have understood the previous program try:

```
10 LET s=0
20 FOR j=1 TO 10
30 CLS
```

```
40 PRINT"ready"
50 FOR i=0 TO RND*50+40
60 NEXT i
70 LET p=23672
80 POKE p+1,0
90 POKE p,0
100 PRINT "go"
110 IF INKEY$="" THEN GOTO 110
120 LET t=PEEK(p)+PEEK(p+1)*256
130 LET t=t/50
140 LET s=s+t
150 NEXT j
160 CLS
170 PRINT"Your average is ";s/i
180 IF s/i>.08 THEN PRINT "Slow"
190 IF s/i>=.05 AND s/i<=.08 THEN PRINT
    "Not bad"
200 IF s/i<.05 THEN PRINT "Well done"
210 IF s/i<.02 THEN PRINT "Very fast"
```

The additional lines at the end of the program calculate your score over ten tries and print out an appropriate message. This routine could be used as the basis for a variety of games. However it is important that you remember that the accuracy of this sort of timing is not very great.

Chapter Nine

STRINGS AND WORDS

It's all too easy to be misled into thinking that computers mainly deal with numbers and complicated or tedious calculations. As you must have realised by now. this is very far from the truth. Indeed, your Spectrum is very good at manipulating text! There are, however, a number of problems about using text to play games that all computers share. Some of these problems have been solved but others take us to the limits of our knowledge of computers. They take us into the area of artificial intelligence.

Strings and things

Before starting on the subject of using strings, a quick recap of how the Spectrum handles strings might be a good idea. The Spectrum distinguishes string variables from others by use of a $ sign after a variable name. For example:

```
10 LET a$="Name"
```

A string can be of any length if it fits into the memory. You can manipulate strings in three ways.

In the first method you can join them together using the + operation. For example:

```
10 LET a$="First Name"
20 LET b$="Last Name"
30 LET a$=a$+b$
40 PRINT a$
```

This program takes the string "First Name" and the string "Last Name" and joins them together to make "First Name Last Name" in the variable a$.

In the second method you can pick out any part of a string using the slicing notation. For example:

```
10 LET a$="abcdefg"
20 PRINT a$(2 TO 5)
```

will print the string abcdefg from the second letter to the
fifth letter, i.e. bcde. You can use the notation a$ (start TO
finish) where "start" and "finish" are replaced by numbers to
mean, the string in a$, from and including the "start" letter, up
to and including the "finish" letter. The Spectrum also allows
certain short forms of the slicing notation.

```
a$ ( TO n) = a$ (1 TO n)
a$ (n)    = a$ (n TO n) i.e. the nth letter
a$ (n TO ) = a$ (n TO LEN(a$))
a$ ( TO ) = a$ (1 TO LEN(a$)) i.e. the whole string
```

The third method of manipulating strings is very clever
indeed. You can change part of a string specified by slicing
notation. For example,

```
10 LET a$="abcdefg"
20 LET a$(2 TO 3)="12345"
30 PRINT a$
```

will change the string abcdefg to a12defg. In other words, the
slicer specifies the part of the string to be changed — the
second letter and the third. It doesn't matter if the string to
the right of the equals sign is bigger than the part to be
changed — the correct number of characters are used starting
from the left. In the example only "12" is used even though
the string is "12345".

As a simple example of string handling try the following:

```
10 INPUT a$
20 LET b$=""
30 FOR I=LEN a$ TO 1 STEP -1
40 LET b$=b$+a$(I)
50 NEXT I
60 PRINT b$
```

This reads in any string and reverses it. Type in the following
sentence 'nuf eb nac margorp siht" to find out what it says.

Notice that the program works by 'stripping' down the input to single letters using the slicer notation and rebuilding it in the reverse order in line 40. You could use this program to send secret messages or simply to teach yourself to speak backwards!

Random words

We discovered how to use random numbers in Chapter Two and how to convert random number into random graphics in Chapter Three. Using the same techniques we can generate random characters. Try the following:

```
10 PRINT CHR$(32+INT(RND*224));
20 GOTO 10
```

You will see the screen fill with random characters something like:

```
MOVE \JM?SQR ØASN PAUSE RNDM TH
EN DPOINT RANDOMIZE LN % FORMAT
ANF<= SAVE Q STOP X1 STEP HO^FN
SQR RETURN COS k]IN CUTAB qw] DI
M Or PEEK . OR WT STOP I<>ASN I
DATA LN 4 OVER NEXT IF + GO SUB
RESTORE DRAW FLASH IN qeT^ASN DR
AW OUT F ERASE AND MERGE CODE 6<
COS ]: AND FOR 8>D1 LIST LN AfLN
/+ THEN ty PAUSE CODE CLEAR Y<U
J<>CHR$ NF DRAW BEEP CVW  TO BRI
GHT CLEAR >9 OL INVERSE qM1 NEW
U] STOP CLEAR X CAT TAB ULN RAND
OMIZE <>PINE INVERSE STOP TABS
DEF FN IYWt] NEW .LN PNINKEY$9xN
NEW GE NEXT NEXT FOR CLEAR ;Y6T
AN OPEN # PRINT l STEP >= LET CO
PY LOAD "STAB AINT DATA NOT STOP
4USR BEEP v OPEN #BHC" DEF FN .
BIN Dg PRINT L7 INVERSE   RETURN
 RVTPIy LET bV5*ATTR BIN I POKE
ZCQ _GI" CONTINUE : CONTINUE CLS
```

The next step is to try to generate random words. If you look at the screen full of random characters generated by the program you should see some words — like GOTO, RND, COPY, etc. These, are, of course nothing more than the Spectrum's BASIC keywords printed on the keyboard. From the Spectrum's point of view these are the same as single

111

characters. They are entered from the keyboard with one key-press and they are stored in one memory location. The only difference is that the key words are expanded into a number of letters when printed. Apart from these keywords it is *very* difficult to generate random words on a computer. If you generate random letters (excluding keywords and graphics) you will be very lucky to see any long words! Try:

```
10 PRINT CHR$(INT(RND*26)+65);
20 GOTO 10
```

```
NCXNZBSBPMRPHVAQTIWXORZKXFQLIPLD
LKOZYFNWPRFMTQTHKBUKQLWGRVSLTARU
EZWWKTGREEBCLYXHNGRQSEYDVYYVOIZX
MRGGCFNJGKVPYMXSJSITGNOBTZLJVBER
QFKIBVQEVIBALPEJUAWAFPIITEIGAVFA
ZRJNFTRBBSIXWMEXGCWTEQOWFVHYHZXJ
CRBDAIFHTFDLTELTLWUNYWPWDOJDYXRM
UHKLAKMLAUMCIVSJLAJLYYQRTLNBJWDU
IJGSJPRPLIKRJWVCUBXFQINQREIYRZIH
OXKANXHMEBWHWDQRGYPKAQJCTJGAZYUF
HVSCAZHJWXSLUZNRVJPXRLPZJNFZDHJD
AFTMMBYHBCUVWIBAIXXWIKAZFVCQNFQH
LZXTADEVQIITBQZNJOEZRSHMNRJCDMPP
NQSONLLWQMNWJJYJLNUVACYHFWQKMTGY
PFDDMZVOMSSBGSMAMWQNOJLNTSIULVPZ
QKUNNRQNEQQRPOYNZMVKEAJNGBQJMZJC
BDMPVXESMTDHVYYYJHTWODDHTCMILBME
KQMYXLGAGGEJVKDEGZDEQEGGRAPAHKCD
ODFTPWTRKCLDAGPQREVKGIMNYUEFOQRM
XRANVZJEJDUACYKXDBWCQGXGMWKMRUDI
BYAUXEPXEYNQSUZRSHJVKWQNQOQWKZHO
TMGUEGXVEGUAFMVYSPUHVQVCEZHQAKBD
```

You might pick out a few three- or four-letter words but not very many when compared to the amount of gibberish produced.

This difficulty with generating random words severely limits the type of word games that a computer can indulge in. For example, if you want to play a number-guessing game, the computer can generate a random number and you can try to guess what it is. In the case of a word-guessing game the computer has no way of generating a random word so the best that you can do is to input a list of words at the start of the game and program the computer to pick a word at random. If you can get someone else to type in the list of possible words or if the list is so long that you cannot remember all the words then you can use this method to play word games.

Hangman

Let's start off by writing a program that will play a simple form of hangman. The following program relies on having someone else to type in a list of words when the player isn't looking.

```
10 LET w$="<"
20 FOR i=1 TO 4
30 INPUT a$
40 LET w$=w$+a$+"<"
50 NEXT i
60 CLS
70 PRINT "HANGMAN"
80 LETr=INT(RND*(LEN w$ - 1)+1)
90 IF w$(r)="<" THEN GOTO 120
100 LET r=r-1
110 GOTO 90
120 LET a$=""
130 LET w$=w$(1 TO r-1)+w$(r+1 TO )
140 IF w$(r)="<" THEN GOTO 170
150 LET a$=a$+w$(r)
160 GOTO 130
170 FOR i=1 TO LEN a$
180 PRINT "*";
190 NEXT i
200 LET h=0
210 PRINT AT 3,0;"Guess a letter"
220 INPUT b$
230 LET k=0
240 FOR i=1 TO LEN a$
250 IF b$(1)=a$(i) THEN LET k=i
260 NEXT i
270 IF k=0 THEN GOTO 210
280 LET a$(k)="*"
```

```
290 LET h=h+1
300 PRINT AT 1,k-1;b$(1)
310 IF h<>LEN a$ THEN GOTO 210
320 PRINT AT 4,0;"Well done"
330 PAUSE 100
340 IF LEN w$>1 THEN GOTO 60
```

The program starts off (lines 10—60) by asking for someone to type in four words. As each word is typed in it is added to a list of words stored in w$. Each word in the list is separated by a "<". If you want to see this add 45 PRINT w$ to the program. After clearing the screen the program then moves on to the hangman game proper. The first thing to be done is to pick a word from the word list at random. This is carried out by lines 80—160. First a random number smaller than the number of characters in the word list (w$) is generated in line 80. This random number can be thought of as "pointing" to the word that has been selected. We then have to transfer the chosen word to another string variable (a$) and delete it from the word list so that it cannot be picked again. This is done by first moving the pointer r back to the first "<" and then transferring everything from there to the next "<" in w$. This is done by lines 90—160. After selecting the target word at random the program goes on to print one "*" for each letter in the word (lines 170—190). Then the program waits for you to type in a guess at line 220. The guess is compared with the word in the FOR loop at lines 240—260. If a match is found then the position of the match is saved in the variable k. Lines 270—310 print the correct letter in the correct position in the word and blank out the guessed letter in the target word with a "*" (line 280). Blanking out the letter with a "*" stops it from being picked up as a correct answer in later guesses. If the number of correct guesses is equal to the length of the target word then you must have guessed the whole word — so a congratulations message is printed (line 320) and the next word, if there is one, is picked at random.

This program uses a number of interesting methods and is well worth studying. If you have enough patience you could increase the number of possible words to something like 100 and then you could type in a list of words yourself because you are hardly likely to be able to remember all the hundred words after a few games of hangman. You can also try to add some graphics and devise a proper scoring method for the number of tries taken to get the correct answer.

Codes and cyphers

Being good at handling both numbers and text, computers are an obvious tool for anyone interested in codes and cyphers. In the Second World War much secret information was discovered by the computer "cracking" coded messages. It is not really possible to use the Spectrum as a code cracker but it can be used as a very good encoding and decoding machine using the properties of the RND and RAND functions described in Chapter Three.

```
10 PRINT "CODER"
20 PRINT "What is your key?"
30 INPUT k
40 RAND k
50 PRINT "Decode or encode (0/1)"
60 INPUT d
70 IF d=0 THEN LET d=-1
80 PRINT "Type your message"
90 INPUT a$
100 FOR i=1 TO LEN a$
110 LET a=CODE a$(i)-64
120 IF a$(i)=" " THEN LET a=0
130 LET a=a + d*INT(RND*59)
140 LET a=ABS(a-INT(a/59)*59)
150 IF a=0 THEN LET a=-32
160 PRINT CHR$(a+64);
170 NEXT i
```

To try the program out decode the following message:

```
UqMhBhULU£x ZeILi
```

115

Run the program and answer 1983 to the question "What is your key". Then answer 0 to the decode/encode question and type in the string of code given above — the decoded message will be printed on the screen.

This program uses the fact that by using the RAND function you can get a specific sequence of random numbers! All you have to do to get exactly the same sequence of numbers is to use the same value when defining RAND. Remember that RAND 0 has a special meaning, it sets the start of the random number generator according to the time since the Spectrum was switched on. This would give you an unknown key — one which could not be repeated in order for later decoding. Zero is therefore the one value that should never be used with this program! The program asks you to input the "key" value you have chosen (line 30) and it is used to start the random number generator (line 40). The same key value has to be used for decoding so if you don't know what key was used to code a message then you cannot decode it. The message typed in line 90 is broken down into letters and each letter is turned into a number using the CODE function. By subtracting 64 from the CODE value we avoid getting graphics characters in the output since graphics characters would be difficult to write down and send to someone else. We code space as 0 at line 120. The rest of the coding works by adding a random number between 0 and 59 and then working out the remainder when you divide the result by 59. The remainder when you divide by 59 lies in the same range as the character codes that we started with, i.e. 0 to 58. To print the resulting characters we use CHR$(a+64) again remembering to correct for the space character (line 150). To decode the message the random number between 0 and 59 is subtracted from the code restoring it to it original pre-coded value. The variable d is set to −1 to decode and to 1 to encode.

This coding program is short but is quite good at producing codes that are difficult to crack. If you haven't got the key then it is virtually impossible to read a Spectrum coded message because the characters are not broken into groups by spaces and the same character can represent different characters at different points in the message.

Numbers as words — a number-guessing game

If you want to play a number-guessing game of the sort that involves guessing individual digits then you have to have a way of matching the guess against the target number and you have to know how to generate a random number with a fixed number of digits. To do this you need to use strings in order to manipulate the individual digits. The number-guessing game given below is quite well known. The computer picks a four digit number at random with no repeated digits. You guess a four digit number and the computer tells you how many of the digits in your number are.

(a) in the target number,
(b) in the same place in the target number.

A digit that is in the same place in the target number is called a place and a digit that is in the target number in a different place is a hit. For example, if the computer had picked 1234 as the target number and you guessed 2035 then you'd have one place — the three — and one hit — the two. The reason for not allowing target numbers with repeated digits is to avoid any difficulty with counting the number of hits.

```
10 LET a$="":LET g=0
20 RAND 0
30 FOR i=1 TO 4
40 LET b$=STR$ INT(RND*10)
50 FOR j=1 TO LEN a$
60 IF a$(j)=b$ THEN GOTO 40
70 NEXT j
80 LET a$=a$+b$
90 NEXT i
100 INPUT b$
110 IF LEN b$<>4 THEN BEEP .5,0 :GOTO 100
120 LET p=0: LET h=0
130 LET g=g+1
140 FOR i=1 TO 4
150 IF a$(i)=b$(i) THEN LET p=p+1
```

```
160 FOR j=1 TO 4
170 IF a$(j)=b$(i) THEN LET h=h+1
180 NEXT j
190 NEXT i
200 LET h=h-p
210 PRINT "Guess ";b$
220 PRINT "Places = ";p,"hits = ";h
230 IF a$<>b$ THEN GOTO 100
240 PRINT "Correct in ";g;" guesses"
```

The random four-digit number is generated in lines 30–90. A random digit (0–9) is generated as a string at line 40 and the digits produced so far are compared with it in lines 50–70. If it's already present we jump back and generate another digit. If it's not already present it is added to the number in line 80. The program waits for a guess at line 100, if it isn't four digits long then it is rejected with a BEEP and the program waits for a correct input. A correct guess is compared for place(s) or hit(s) in lines 140–190. Checking for a place is easy and is done by comparing both numbers, digit by digit in line 150 and adding one to p for every match. Checking for a hit is slightly trickier and requires an extra FOR loop at lines 160 to 180. Each digit in the guess is compared with *every other* digit in the target and one is added to h for every match. This hit count includes digits that are also in the right place so we have to subtract p to get a corrected hit count (line 200). Numbers of places and hits are printed at line 220 and line 230 checks to see if you've guessed the number. In the following sample of output, the computer's number was 8340 and it took the player five tries to guess it.

```
Guess 1234
Places = 0          hits = 2
Guess 0987
Places = 0          hits = 2
Guess 1279
Places = 0          hits = 0
Guess 3480
Places = 1          hits = 3
Guess 8340
Places = 4          hits = 0
Correct in 5 guesses
```

No instructions or messages are included in the program and it would be much improved by adding more sound and colour — but this is left to you. But even as it is, this game can be addictive so play with care!

Chapter Ten

ADVANCED GRAPHICS

It is often the case that a program is easier to write or more effective if a mixture of high and low resolution graphics is employed. However, this brings with it the difficulty of matching up the two co-ordinate systems. The following program is an example of just such a situation.

Mixing resolutions — depth-charge game

The idea behind this game is to animate two ships — one a surface vessel and the other a submarine — and allow the first one to "drop" a depth charge on the other. The ships are easy to display using low resolution graphics but the depth charge is best done using high resolution graphics. If you followed the discussion in Chapter Six you should be able to see how to write this program for yourself. To animate the two ships we could use the general method of printing a shape at the first position, blanking it out and reprinting it, moved on a little. However as the ships are going to move horizontally in a straight line we can use a trick to simplify the programming. Try the following program:

```
10 FOR x=0 TO 30
20 PRINT AT 3,x;"[8]*";
30 NEXT x
```

You should see an asterisk move from left to right at the top of the screen. Notice that this program combines the reprinting of the asterisk with the blanking out of the previous position by including a blank in the moving "object". In general, it is always possible to use this technique. All you have to do is to ensure that whenever the "object" is printed it includes enough blanks around it to "wipe out" the old version. In practice, this is too difficult unless the object is moving in a straight line. (For another example of this method see the bat in "Squash".)

Other specific problems with the depth-charge game are deciding when the submarine is hit and producing a suitable "explosion" to remove it from the screen, but everything to do with the depth charge itself is complicated by the fact that it is produced using high resolution graphics and the ship and submarine are produced using low resolution graphics. The complete program is listed below. (Remember that graphics characters are indicated by square brackets around the letter on the key that you would press to produce it.)

```
10 LET mc=0
20 LET hc=0
30 LET f=0
40 LET h=0
50 LET xs=0
60 GOSUB 600
70 LET x=0
80 LET ys=INT(RND*5)+15
90 LET y=2
100 GOSUB 200
110 PRINT AT 0,0;"Hits=";hc;TAB(10);"Misses=";mc
120 IF f=0 THEN LET xd=8*x:LET yd=140
130 REM f is the fire indicator
140 IF INKEY$="f" AND f=0 THEN LET f=1
150 IF f=1 THEN GOSUB 300
160 GOSUB 400
170 IF h=0 THEN GOTO 100
180 GOSUB 500
190 GOTO 30

200 PRINT AT y,x;"[8][^3][^8][^3][^3]";
210 LET x=x+1
220 IF x>25 THEN LET x=0
230 IF x=0 THEN PRINT AT y,26;"[8][8][8][8]";
240 RETURN
```

```
300 PLOT INVERSE 1,xd,yd
310 LET yd=yd-4
320 PLOT xd,yd
330 REM hit?
340 IF yd<16 THEN LET f=0:LET mc=mc+1
350 IF f=0 THEN PLOT INVERSE 1,xd,yd
360 IF ABS(xd-8*xs-24)>24 THEN RETURN
370 IF ABS(yd-175+8*ys)>8 THEN RETURN
380 LET h=1
390 RETURN

400 PRINT AT ys,xs;"[8][^2][^3][^3]";
410 LET xs=xs+RND
420 IF xs>28 THEN LET xs=0
430 IF xs=0 THEN PRINT AT ys,28; "[8][8][8][8]";
440 RETURN

500 LET hc=hc+1
510 FOR i=1 TO 20
520 PRINT AT ys,xs;"[6][^4][4][5]";
530 PRINT AT ys,xs;"[8][8][8][8]"
540 NEXT i
550 RETURN

600 CLS
610 FOR i=0 TO 31
620 PRINT AT 3,i;"[^3]";
630 PRINT AT 21,i;"[3]";
640 NEXT i
650 RETURN
```

The program starts by initialising variables and drawing the
sea and sea bed using subroutine 600. The depth of the submarine is selected at random by line 80. Subroutine 200 plots
the surface ship at location x,y and subroutine 400 plots the
submarine at location xs,ys. The submarine moves in the same

direction as the surface ship and the amount that it moves is random (line 410). The depth charge is released by pressing the "F" key and line 140 checks for this, using the INKEY$ function. When the depth charge has been dropped the variable f is set to one and the location of the depth charge is then stored in xd,yd. Subroutine 300 is responsible for keeping track of where the depth charge is and keeping it moving. Notice that, as the depth charge is produced using the PLOT command and the ships are produced using PRINT AT, there is a problem with comparing co-ordinates. PLOT works with a screen 256 by 176 and PRINT AT works with a 32 by 22 screen. Obviously xd and yd are measured from the bottom of the screen and y is measured from the top! All this makes starting the depth charge off and deciding if it has hit the submarine more difficult than you might expect. Lines 120 and 130 keep xd and yd set to the same location as the surface ship, so that when the depth charge is dropped it starts falling from the current position of the surface ship. Lines 360 and 370 check to see if the depth charge has hit the submarine. Notice that to compare the two x co-ordinates it is enough to multiply by eight but to compare the two y co-ordinates you have to subtract 8*ys from 175. The rest of the program is fairly straightforward but notice the way that the submarine is "destroyed" in lines 510 to 540. This might prove useful in other games.

Screen layout

Everything that is displayed on the TV screen is stored in the Spectrum's memory. Knowledge of where and how the screen is stored can be useful and can actually suggest new ways of using graphics. As hinted in Chapter Two, information about what should be displayed on the screen is divided into two parts — the ink-paper dot memory and the attribute memory. The ink-paper dot memory stores information as to whether each dot in the 256 x 176 screen grid is an ink dot or a paper dot. The attribute memory is used to store the current ink colour, paper colour, brightness and flash state for each character position. To make things easier we will look at each in turn.

The ink-paper dot area of memory starts at memory location 16384 and goes up to 22527. Each memory location can store the state of a total of eight dots. The way that memory locations correspond to screen positions is particularly complicated. Starting with the top row of dots, the first eight (on the left) are stored in the first memory location. The next eight are stored in the next and so on to the end of the row. That is the first 32 memory locations hold the top row of dots on the screen. Notice that these 32 memory locations also correspond to the 32 character printing positions. In other words, each memory location stores the top row of eight dots of a character location. If everything was simple, the next 32 memory locations would hold the second row of dots. Unfortunately this is not the case. In fact it is the first row of dots making up the second line of characters that is stored next, i.e. the ninth row of dots counting from the top of the screen. Then the first row of the third line of characters is stored and so on to the first row of the eighth line of characters. Then the pattern is repeated with the second row of the eight character lines and so on. If this wasn't enough, the whole pattern is repeated three times to store the three blocks of eight characters that make up the screen (i.e.

24 lines including the input area).

This storage pattern is difficult to understand from a description but if you try the following program you will see the pattern in "action".

```
10 FOR i=16384 TO 22527
20 POKE i,255
30 NEXT i
```

This stores a line of ink dots (255=BIN 11111111) in each memory location in the screen area starting at the beginning (16384) and continuing on up consecutively. The order that you see the horizontal line appear should be as predicted above.

To make any use of the knowledge about how the screen is stored you need to be able to find any screen position in memory. That is given a line, column and character row number you need a formula that will give you the memory location that it is stored in. The following is rather complicated but it does fit the bill,

$$\text{memory location} = 16384 + 2048 * INT(L) + 32 * (L - 8 * INT(L/8)) + 256 * R + C$$

where L is the line number, C is the column number and R is the character row number (all starting from zero). So if you wanted to know what dot pattern was stored in the third row of the second character in the third line, R would be 2, C

125

would be 1 and L would be 2. To see this formula in action try the following:

```
10 DEF FNs(L,c,r)=16384+2048*INT(L/8)
   +32*(L-8*INT(L/8))+256*r+c
20 CLS
30 FOR n=0 TO 7
40 FOR i=0 TO 31
50 FOR j=0 TO 23
60 POKE FNs(j,i,n),255
70 NEXT j
80 NEXT i
90 NEXT n
```

This fills the screen with short horizontal lines working vertically from the left. Even after all this work it has to be admitted that the complexity of the screen storage format probably deters any direct access to it using PEEK and POKE.

Now we come to the attributes area of memory. This is considerably easier to make sense of. Starting at 22528 and extending up to 23295 there is one memory location for every character location on the screen. The way that character locations are associated with memory locations is also a lot easier. The first character location on the top line corresponds to the first memory location, the second to the second and so on to the end of the line. After this the first character on the second line corresponds to the 33rd memory location and so on down the screen. So to work out the memory location corresponding to the character in line L and column C we simply have to use.

$$22528+32*L+C$$

(Once again remembering to count lines and columns starting from zero.) Each memory location stores the current values for the attributes of each character location. The way that these attributes are stored will be discussed later but for the moment try the following program.

```
10 FOR i=1 TO 32*21
20 PRINT CHR$(INT(RND*26+65));
30 NEXT i
40 FOR x=22528 TO 23295
50 POKE x,INT(RND*256)
60 NEXT x
70 GOTO 40
```

The first part of the program, lines 10 to 30, fills the screen with random characters. The second part changes the contents of the attribute memory to random values starting at the top left hand corner and working down and across the screen. There are two things to notice about the output from this program. Firstly, the order in which the character locations are changed is governed by the way in which the memory locations correspond to character locations. Secondly, notice that only the attributes of what is stored on the screen are altered. In other words, the characters that are displayed are left unaltered — they simply change colour or start to flash. You should be able to see that this could be useful if you wanted to present a screen display and then change its colour without having to reprint the whole thing.

The only thing that we still need to know is the exact way that what is stored in the attributes area of memory determines the attributes of what is shown on the screen. This is solved by the following formula which calculates the value that has to be stored in a memory location to produce the desired attributes,

128*FLASH+64*BRIGHT+8*PAPER+INK

where FLASH and BRIGHT are either 0 or 1 depending on whether the character location is to be flashing or bright, and PAPER and INK are the colour codes of the required paper and ink colours. So if you wanted a flashing, normal contrast, black paper, red ink character you would store

128*1+64*0+8*0+2

i.e. 130 in the correct attribute memory location.

To make life slightly easier, the Spectrum has a function that returns the attribute value for any character location without having to work out the address to PEEK. The function is:

ATTR(line,column)

The only problem is that you are still left the problem of decoding the value that ATTR returns to discover, for example, what the paper colour is. To help with this problem the following list of BASIC statements can be used:

```
flash=INT(ATTR(line,col)/128))
bright=INT((ATTR(line,col)-INT(ATTR(line,col)/128)*128)/64)
paper=INT((ATTR(line,col)-INT(ATTR(line,col)/64*64)/8)
ink=ATTR(line,col)-INT(ATTR(line,col)/8)*8
```

SCREEN$ and POINT

After the discussion of how everything concerning the screen display is stored in memory, you will realise that it is fairly easy to find out what colour something is. Finding out what it is that is actually displayed is, however, much more difficult. Even if the formula for the screen address is employed, all you can find out by PEEKing the screen is what the eight rows of dots that make up the character are. And while it is one thing to know the pattern of dots that makes up a letter "A" it is

128

quite another to try to find out what letter a particular pattern of dots corresponds to.

Fortunately ZX BASIC comes to the rescue with a function SCREEN$ (line,column). This will take the eight rows of dots that appear in any character location and try to match them against the patterns of dots that appear in the character generator table (see Chapter Seven). If the pattern matches a character in the table then SCREEN$ returns that character as a string. If no match can be found then SCREEN$ returns the null string as an answer. The only thing that you have to notice is that it is only the pattern of dots that matters, not how it was created. For example, you could make the pattern of dots for a letter "A" using PLOT commands and as long as they were in the right place within a character location then SCREEN$ would return "A". Another quirk about the way SCREEN$ works is that it doesn't distinguish between a character and its inverse. This means that a blank (CHR$(32), the solid graphics block [^8] and the empty graphics block [8] all make SCREEN$ return a blank! (An example of using SCREEN$ is given in the Maze program that follows.)

There is also a solution supplied to the much easier problem of determining whether any particular point on the screen is an ink or a paper point.

POINT(x,y)

is zero if the point in question (i.e. at x,y) is paper and one if it is ink. In practice it is unusual for what happens in a program to depend on a single point so POINT isn't used as much as you might expect.

Maze game

The maze game is a Spectrum version of a game found on many a popular micro. The basic idea is that you have control over the movements of an asterisk that starts out in the bottom right hand corner of the screen and the object of the game is to get it into the top left hand corner. Sounds easy doesn't it! The catch is that your way is blocked by a randomly changing pattern of dark squares and the skill is to steer your way as quickly as possible through any openings before they close.

Before looking at the completed program try to think how you might go about writing it. The problem is obviously knowing when your way is blocked. Do you really have to record the x and y co-ordinate of every dark square on the screen?

```
10 INK 2:PAPER 6:BORDER 1
20 INPUT "Difficulty level 1-9 ?";d
30 IF d<1 OR d>9 THEN GOTO 20
40 LET d1=d/10
50 CLS
60 GOSUB 100
70 GOSUB 300
80 GOSUB 500

100 POKE USR "a"+0,BIN 01010101
110 POKE USR "a"+1,BIN 10101010
120 POKE USR "a"+2,BIN 01010101
130 POKE USR "a"+3,BIN 10101010
140 POKE USR "a"+4,BIN 01010101
150 POKE USR "a"+5,BIN 10101010
160 POKE USR "a"+6,BIN 01010101
170 POKE USR "a"+7,BIN 10101010
180 RETURN

200 LET c$=SCREEN$(y,x)
210 RETURN

300 REM setup maze
310 GOSUB 1000
320 FOR i=1 TO 20*d+40
330 LET x=RND*29+1
340 LET y=RND*19+1
350 PRINT AT y,x;"[a]";
360 NEXT i
```

```
370 PRINT AT 1,1;"$";
380 PRINT AT 20,30;"*";
400 RETURN

500 LET xc=30
510 LET yc=20
520 LET m=0
530 LET x=xc
540 LET y=yc
550 LET a$=INKEY$
560 GOSUB 900
570 IF a$="" THEN GOTO 550
580 IF a$="5" THEN LET x=xc-1
590 IF a$="8" THEN LET x=xc+1
600 IF a$="6" THEN LET y=yc+1
610 IF a$="7" THEN LET y=yc-1
620 GOSUB 200
630 IF c$="$" THEN GOTO 800
640 IF c$<>" " THEN BEEP .1,10:GOTO 530
650 PRINT AT yc,xc;" ";
660 LET xc=x
670 LET yc=y
680 PRINT AT yc,xc;"*";
690 LET m=m+1
700 GOTO 530

800 CLS
810 PRINT AT 0,2;"You have taken ";m;" moves"
820 PRINT "Another game y/n"
830 INPUT a$
840 IF a$(1)="y" THEN RUN
850 IF a$(1)<>"n" THEN GOTO 820
860 STOP

900 IF RND>d1 THEN RETURN
910 LET c$=" "
```

```
920 IF RND>.5 THEN LET c$="[a]"
930 PRINT AT RND*19+1,RND*29+1;c$
940 PRINT AT 1,1;"$";
950 RETURN

1000 FOR i=0 TO 31
1010 PRINT AT 0,i;INK 0;"[a]";AT 21,i;"[a]";
1020 NEXT i
1030 FOR i=0 TO 21
1040 PRINT AT i,0;INK 0;"[a]";AT i,31;"[a]";
1050 NEXT i
1060 RETURN
```

The program starts off by asking for the difficulty level, d. This governs how many squares are used to block your way. This information is used by subroutine 300 to construct the initial maze. The details of this are straightforward. First a call to subroutine 1000 draws a border around the maze using the graphics character defined by subroutine 100. Next a PRINT AT is used to print the graphics block [A] at random points on the screen. Before leaving the subroutine a "$" sign is printed in the top left hand corner to represent the target position for the asterisk which is printed in the bottom right hand corner. The game proper begins with a call to subroutine 500. After some initialisation, the arrow keys are checked by line 550 and the values of xc and yc, the present position of the asterisk, are updated into x and y, the intended position of the asterisk, according to which arrow key has been pressed. The next problem is to decide if the intended position is legal. If it contains only a blank character then it is ok to move the asterisk there. If it contains any other character then the move must be rejected. Subroutine 200 is called at line 620 to examine the screen and find out what is at x,y (using the SCREEN$ function). The character at the screen location is returned in c$. If this is a "$" then control is passed to line 800 to finish the game. Unless this condition is found, line 640 checks to make sure that c$ is a blank. If it is anything else then the move is rejected with a BEEP. If it is a blank, however, then the old asterisk's position is blanked at line 650 and the new asterisk is printed at line 680. The move count m is incremented and the move logic is repeated by line 700. The only details that we haven't discussed are subroutine 900, that adds and removes blockages, and lines 800 to 860, that print the results of a game and asks if you want to play again. Both of these should be easy to understand. Notice how the use of SCREEN$ to discover what is in the proposed printing position also stops the asterisk being "driven" off the sides of the screen without having to use extra IF statements. Because the maze is surrounded by a non-blank border the move logic will not allow you to cross it!

After studying the techniques presented in this chapter, you should be able to make use of PEEK,POKE and SCREEN$ to produce animated graphics to good effect. As an exercise it would be a good idea to change the squash program given earlier to use SCREEN$ to detect if the ball is about to hit the bat or the side walls.

Scrolling graphics

So far we have accumulated a wide range of methods for producing moving graphics but there is still one problem that is difficult to solve — making many things move at once. In general it is not possible to make more than one or two things move at any speed on the Spectrum using BASIC. However there is one exception to this. Try the following program:

```
10 CLS
20 POKE 23692,255
30 PRINT AT 21,RND*31;"*"''
40 GOTO 20
```

Line 30 causes the screen to scroll because of the double apostrophe at the end and this moves the entire screen one line vertically. The time that this takes is not dependent on how many things are moved! Line 20 is necessary to suppress the "Scroll?" appearing (see Chapter Seven for details). The difficulty with scrolling graphics is not moving things but making them stay still! If you print something on the top line after each scroll then it appears to be stationary in a stream of moving asterisks. Add

```
35 PRINT AT 0,16;"V";
```

to the previous program and you have the start of a "pilot a spaceship through the stars" game!

Ski run game

To show how powerful scrolling graphics can be try the ski run program given below:

```
10 RAND 0
20 LET b$="<>"
30 CLS
40 DIM c(26,2)
50 GOSUB 5000
60 GOSUB 1000
70 LET t=0
80 LET p=0
90 LET x=16
100 GOSUB 2000
```

(Please note that in line 20 etc., it is important that you type a "less than" symbol, followed immediately by a "greater than" symbol rather than an "inequality sign".)

134

```
110 GOTO 4000

1000 FOR i=1 TO 25
1010 LET c(i,1)=INT(RND*5)+5
1020 LET c(i,2)=INT(RND*25)+4
1030 NEXT i
1040 LET c(1,1)=21
1050 RETURN

2000  POKE 23692,255:PRINT AT 21,c(1,2);">";
2010 LET k=1
2020 LET j=0
2030 LET m=0
2040 LET i=2
2050 LET s=0
2060 LET s=s+1
2070 LET t=t+1
2080 PRINT AT 21,0"
2090 GOSUB 3000
2100 IF s<>c(i,1) THEN GOTO 2060
2110 POKE 23692,255:PRINT AT 21,c(i,2);b$(j+1);
2120 LET j=NOT j
2130 LET i=i+1
2140 IF i<26 THEN GOTO 2050
2150 FOR i=1 TO 23
2160 LET t=t+1
2170 POKE 23692,255:PRINT AT 21,0"
2180 GOSUB 3000
2190 NEXT i
2200 RETURN

3000 LET a$=INKEY$
3010 IF a$="5" THEN LET x=x-1
3020 IF a$="8" THEN LET x=x+1
3030 PRINT AT 0,x;"*";
```

135

```
3040 IF t<>c(m+1,1) THEN RETURN
3050 LET t=0
3060 LET m=m+1
3070 LET k=NOT k
3080 IF NOT k AND (x-c(m,2)) > 0 THEN RETURN
3090 IF k AND (x-c(m,2)) < 0 THEN RETURN
3100 LET p=p+1
3110 BEEP .05,20:PRINT "h"
3120 RETURN

4000 PRINT
4010 PRINT "You hit ";p;" gates"
4020 PRINT "Do you want to try again ?";
4030 INPUT a$
4040 PRINT a$
4050 IF a$(1)="n" THEN STOP
4060 IF a$<>"y" THEN GOTO 4020
4070 PRINT "Same course ?";
4080 INPUT a$
4090 PRINT a$
4100 IF a$(1)="y" THEN GOTO 70
4110 IF a$(1)<>"n" THEN GOTO 4070
4120 GOTO 60

5000 CLS
5010 PRINT
5020 PRINT TAB 8;"S K I   R U N"
5030 PRINT TAB 8;"--------------"
5040 PRINT
5050 PRINT "You have to ski down a course"
5060 PRINT "of 25 flags."
5070 PRINT
5080 PRINT "You must pass to the left of"
5090 PRINT "< and to the right of >"
5100 PRINT
```

```
5110 PRINT "You can move to the right and"
5120 PRINT "left by pressing the arrow keys"
5130 PRINT "(5 and 8)"
5140 PRINT
5150 PRINT "press any key to start"
5160 IF INKEY$="" THEN GOTO 5160
5170 CLS
5180 RETURN
```

Although the idea that lies behind this program is simple enough and based on the idea of scrolling graphics, it takes some quite tricky "book keeping" to keep track of where everything is on the screen. First, instructions for the game are given by subroutine 5000 and then a random course is constructed by subroutine 1000. This is done by generating two random numbers — the distance, in number of scrolls, between each successive gate and its horizontal position. The game starts by a call to subroutine 4000 that prints the first gate and begins to scroll the screen toward the skier represented by an asterisk. The difficult part is that after a certain number of scrolls, contained in $c(2,1)$, the next gate is printed and after 21 scrolls (remember, there are 22 useable lines on the screen) the first gate reaches the skier. At this point the position of the skier is checked to see that he is on the correct side of the gate. You should be able to see that following this logic it is possible to work out when each gate passes the skier and thus keep track of the number of gates correctly passed. The details of this are easier to program (lines 2000 to 3120) than they are to explain, so over to you!

Conclusion

You can use the techniques described in this chapter to produce some very clever graphics. For example, you could try to combine the methods of scrolling graphics with SCREEN$ graphics or use PEEKing and POKEing in the attribute area to produce moving colours. However, after any amount of trickery it is hard to avoid the conclusion that BASIC is just not fast enough to make "arcade" quality games possible, let alone easy. For the solution I am afraid that there is no choice but to leave BASIC and learn machine code — however that is another story.

* * * * *

CASSETTE TAPES

Ramsoft, P.O. Box 6, Richmond, North Yorkshire DL10 4HL, England

As well as explaining programming techniques, this book also contains lots of programs that are fun to play, interesting to watch or useful to have available. So we've taken twenty of them and put them onto a single cassette tape.

The programs contained on the tape are: Heads and Tails; Kaleidoscopes; Squash; Digital Clock; Hangman; Arrows Game; Depth Charge; Dice; Symmetry; Lunar Lander; Chess Clock; Coder; Big Letters; Ski; Pontoon; Dixie; Cannon-ball; Reaction Time Game; Mastermind; Maze.

Write directly to the address given above for further details and an order form. Please enclose a stamped addressed envelope.

PLEASE NOTE: The Publishers of this book are in no way responsible for the manufacture or supply of these tapes and all enquiries must be sent directly to Ramsoft.

The contents of the tapes may be subject to change without further notice.